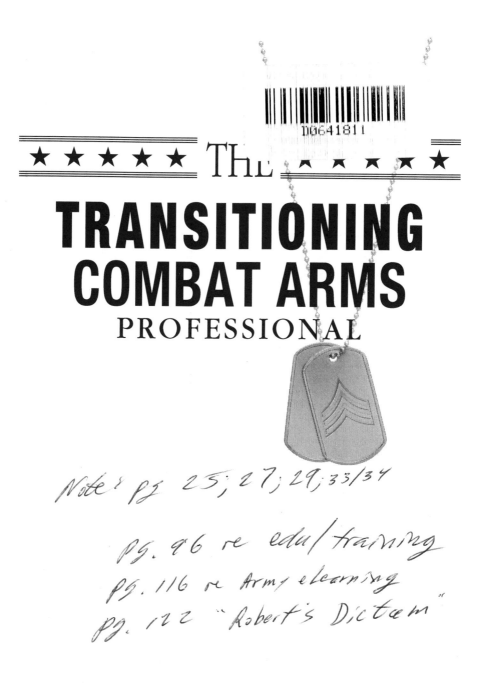

★★★★★ The ★★★★★
TRANSITIONING
COMBAT ARMS
PROFESSIONAL

Note: pg 25; 27; 29; 33/34

pg. 96 re edu/training
pg. 116 re Army elearning
pg. 122 "Robert's Dictum"

THE TRANSITIONING MILITARY SERIES

★ ★ ★ ★ ★ THE ★ ★ ★ ★ ★
TRANSITIONING
COMBAT ARMS
PROFESSIONAL

JAY HICKS
Lieutenant Colonel, United States Army, Retired

JACK TILLEY
12th Sergeant Major of the Army, Retired

GR8TRANSITIONS4U, INC.

Published by GR8TRANSITIONS4U
GR8TRANSITIONS4U (USA) Inc.
PO Box 56084
St. Petersburg, FL 33732

Hicks, Jay
THE TRANSITIONING COMBAT ARMS PROFESSIONAL
Includes End Notes
ISBN 978-0- 9864376-6-3

Printed in the United States of America

Book design by Tamara Parsons
Kensington Type & Graphics

*Dedicated to the
Soldiers and Marines of the
United States of America.*

Table of Contents

Foreword

Preface

CHAPTER 1   *Introduction*. 1

CHAPTER 2   *Know Yourself`* 17

CHAPTER 3   *Targeting Your Next Career* 63

CHAPTER 4   *The Market Place*. 123

CHAPTER 5   *The Right Fit* 155

APPENDIX A   *Certification & License* 171

APPENDIX B   *Salary Considerations* 176

APPENDIX C   *Personal Strategic Road Map*. 178

Acknowledgements 179

End Notes 183

Foreword

"HIRE VETS!" "VETERANS MAKE THE BEST EMPLOYEES!" "HIRE LEADERS – HIRE VETERANS." "JOINING FORCES." Slogans and programs addressing the benefits (and challenges) of hiring America's veterans abound. A quick internet search for "veteran hiring organization" or "veteran job listings" reveals countless responses. There's no shortage of advice, but good advice from people who know what they are talking about can be hard to come by.

So, how does a transitioning Service member, particularly one who served as a combat arms professional, wade through the seemingly endless amount of available information concerning finding employment after the military? For those who leave the armed forces with a civilian-related technical or administrative skill, the transition may not be any easier, but it is, perhaps, more well-defined than for those whose military service may not be directly transferrable (or understandable) to the private sector. This book, The Transitioning Combat Arms Professional seeks to offer useful insights, recommendations and proven practices to aid those with what some might characterize as "hard-core" military skills – infantry, armor, artillery, and others – make a successful move from uniformed service to another set of opportunities. Let's face it, the demand for tank drivers or machine gunners in the private sector is pretty limited!

The authors, Lieutenant Colonel (Retired) Jay Hicks and Sergeant Major of the Army (Retired) Jack Tilley, have both experienced highly successful military careers and subsequent transitions to civilian life. Their personal insights, combined with the personal examples of many others, chart a proven path for those now making this transition. Each person who has returned to civilian life, be it after two years or 40 years in uniform, whether active duty, National Guard or Reserve, has unique experiences; this is not a "one size fits all" model. If it were that simple, this book would not be necessary. But, the fact is that few employers, in either the for profit, non-profit or public sectors, are able to readily understand the skills, attributes and experience of combat arms professionals. Consequently, you need to help prospective employers better understand your skill set, your capabilities, your potential. That's what this book is about.

The Transitioning Combat Arms Professional is not a one-time read book. Use it as a reference during your journey from military service to your next career. As you learn and grow, refer back to the book to refine your understanding of yourself, the market place, and the opportunities that best match your abilities and desires. You've succeeded in uniform by understanding the environment in which you have operated, and then adapting to changes as they occur. That experience will serve you well in this new endeavor.

Good luck in your transition! Know that you are not alone. Be proud of your service. And, as you become successful in your post-military endeavors, look for opportunities to aid others as they depart the military. The camaraderie that gave you strength while in the Service doesn't end the day you take off your uniform.

And, most of all, thank you for choosing to serve our nation.

General Carter Ham
General, U.S. Army Retired
President & CEO, Association of the United States Army

CONGRATULATIONS! If you have picked up this book, you are probably preparing to transition from the military. You may be unaware of the value and significance of the experience gained from your military Service. This book will assist you with military transitional challenges and provide some good common sense guidance as you deal with the inevitable uncertainties along your journey. By using the tactics given in this book you will gain a professional advantage, setting into motion a course of action that will reduce transitional stress and create a satisfying and financially-lucrative outcome.

Millions of Service members have transitioned -- now it is your turn. This book, along with its companion guide, will organize the chaos associated with transition, ease your concerns, and increase your confidence. Download your free companion guide from GR8Transitions4U.com. The guide contains copies of reusable assessments, charting forms, and a Personal Strategic Roadmap, as well as process details and examples for using the forms. Keep the companion guide nearby to use when performing your personal assessments to chart your strategic roadmap. Leverage your military experience.

Good luck in your transition!

THE TRANSITIONING
COMBAT ARMS
PROFESSIONAL

Preface

WHEN I JOINED THE ARMY IN 1966, I HAD NO IDEA OF THE PHENOMENAL JOURNEY THAT LAY AHEAD. Just as you, we all worked hard as a team and I was fortunate enough to eventually ended up as Sergeant Major of the Army. I am thankful for my success, but I wanted to provide some advice for you as you begin your transition.

It is essential that you begin your transition early and have the right tools. This book will provide a tremendous head start, if you have yet to make up your mind what you are going to do after the service. You will be informed on numerous career fields and potential paths for your next career. Use the book and companion guide and perform the required self-analysis.

Being well informed on your objective establishes a solid platform for success, and this book provides that foundation. This book provides a roadmap and is a virtual template for success for you during your military transition. Use this book and feel confident that you are holding in your hands a bridge to "what right looks like."

Jack L. Tilley
12th Sergeant Major of the Army
Retired

Introduction

YOU ARE ABOUT TO EMBARK ON ONE OF THE GREATEST JOURNEYS OF YOUR LIFE. Through the military, you have served your country well. You have suffered hardships and endured challenges that most of your fellow citizens will never experience. Now it is time to move on to your next experience; your job transition into civilian world! Transitioning from the military is challenging and you must ensure that you are well prepared. Benjamin Franklin once stated, "By failing to prepare, you are preparing to fail." You have already made a great step in the right direction by beginning to read this book. Now it is your turn to enjoy the virtues of selecting and pursuing a lucrative post-military career. It's time to do what you were meant to do. All you must do is determine the direction of your employment desires.

Got Dreams?

Security guard, police officer, deputy sheriff are all great jobs for the Combat Arms professional after military Service. Numerous websites, books, and articles have stated that you would be perfect in the career fields of security and law enforcement. Maybe this is what you always wanted to do after the military. It is an honorable profession. But, are you tired of hearing that you would make a good security guard? You do not have to settle for this line of work. If something way back in the recesses of your mind is pulling at you, tugging at you because you desire more, then keep reading.

> *"A dream doesn't become reality through magic; it takes sweat, determination and hard work."*
>
> ~ Colin Powell

You have spent years in the Service of our country. Now, is your time! It is the time to do what you are good at and what you enjoy. What you do best, is exactly what the world needs you to do.

You may be saying, "This guy doesn't know what he is talking about," or "I have to support my family," or "I don't have the skills for anything else and the military is all I know." Others may say, "I'm just an infantryman," or "All I know is tanks."

You may have heard, "Follow what you love and then the money will follow." That is not always the case. However, you do not have to settle for less. There is a great big world out there, ready for exploration. It is time to stretch; spread your wings and try something else. Now the time has come for you to think about you and this book will help you with that.

> *"I was a born troublemaker and might as well earn a living at it."*
>
> ~ Bill Mauldin
> *(WWII Cartoonist)*

Within the pages of this book, you will find success stories, roadmaps, assessments, career mapping and hopefully thought-provoking text. This book is designed to assist your thinking about what you were meant to do. You have much more capability than you can imagine. You just need to think about what it is that you have always wanted to do.

A recent book by Todd Henry, entitled "Die Empty," states that the most expensive piece of property in the world, is the graveyard. That's because there are countless dreams and an untold number of enterprises buried there alongside the dead. The premise is that you do not want to go to your grave, never having pursued your dreams.

There are no dishonorable jobs, unless they are illegal, immoral, or against the law. A famous general, when hired to mop floors in a soft drink factory as a young man stated, "If I'm going to mop floors, I'll be the best darn floor mopper you ever saw!"[1] You take pride in what you have done for the military, and you should. You have performed superbly. But now, reach back and reflect upon your passions. Where is your passion? What do you think you would love to do? Law? Entrepreneurship? Operations management? Teacher or instructor? Physical trainer? Automotive mechanic? Artist? Ministry? Now it's your time!

Let's explore your known and potential attraction towards numerous occupations. Then you will be able to move toward these occupations with some coaching and direction. To do this successfully, the first thing you need to do is spend some time assessing what you were meant to do. We will help you with that.

Change and Transition

Nothing is constant, except change. The world we live in is changing at a very rapid pace. You as an individual are changing, growing, learning and gaining knowledge every day. Change consultant William Bridges, created the Transition

> "It isn't the changes that do you in; it's the transitions."
> ~ William Bridges

Model in his book "Managing Transitions." The main strength of the model is that it focuses on transition, not change. The difference between these two terms is subtle but important. Change is something that happens to people, even if they do not agree with it. Transition, on the other hand, is internal; it is what happens in people's minds as they go through change. Change can happen very quickly, while transition usually occurs more slowly.[2]

Our lives are full of change. Your military transition may prove to be one of your greatest challenges and achievements. How will you handle your transition? Are you going to be frustrated and tossed about like a boat in a storm? People are often quite uncomfortable with change for many understandable reasons. This can lead to resistance and opposition during the transition. To transition successfully you must embrace your personal change and mentally take charge of your transition. Use your knowledge and experience to help embrace your personal and professional change.

> *"Change is never painful. Only resistance to change is painful."*
>
> ~ Buddha

In today's challenging work environment, modern workers must be flexible, embrace change and continually transition in order to remain viable. The good news is your military experience has instilled the ability to adapt to ever changing environments. This flexibility will serve you well as you respond to change. How will you embrace the change that is coming to your personal and professional life? What actions will you take to enable your successful transition? As you depart the Service, remember to embrace the associated changes, but remain focused on your transition.

Companies are constantly seeking qualified candidates who have the ability to change and grow with the organization. If you are ready to adapt to this rapidly changing environment, this is all good news for you.

Transition Strategy

The time has come for you to transition. Your military experience tells you that every major operation needs a good strategy and a plan. You have performed planning at the personal and organizational level before. Now it is time to generate your own personal strategic transition plan or roadmap.

The ability to plan and execute a personal strategy is potentially your greatest attribute. Strategy sets your direction and establishes your priorities in terms of goals. It defines your view of success and prioritizes activities that will make this view a reality. Strategy helps you

> *"Artillery adds dignity, to what would otherwise be an ugly brawl"*
>
> ~ Frederick the Great

know what you should work on and what should be addressed first. Once goals are set, tactics are used to achieve these goals. While transitioning from the military, start framing your approach by reflecting on questions like:

- What are my capabilities?
- What are my qualities that an employer would seek?
- How do I chart a course of action allowing me to unleash my superb capabilities as quickly as possible after transitioning from the military?
- Do I know what career is best suited for me?
- How do I get from where I am to where I want to be?

The Personal Strategic Roadmap, outlined in Chapter 5 of this book, assists in answering these types of questions, while offering guidance during your career change by establishing obtainable goals and objectives.

Why this Book is for You

In the midst of your transition, like the fog of war, you may feel unbalanced and confused. It is easy to get lost. It becomes painfully obvious if you have not connected all of the dots correctly. You can increase the success of your transition by understanding and successfully applying the basics presented in this book. Careful planning and execution are critical. Just like a military mission, plan well and execute brilliantly. Therefore, understanding your Combat Arms and other skills in relation to commercial career fields is vital. This book and the associated web site aid in understanding how to prepare for and secure work in a civilian setting; all the while developing your transition roadmap. Practical advice on how to take the skill sets you have already obtained in the military and applying them to your next career will increase your confidence and help you to become a skilled and trusted commercial professional. If your transition has already begun, this book may provide answers to critical information you may have missed.

> *"I'm convinced that the infantry is the group in the Army which gives more and gets less than anybody else."*
>
> ~ Bill Mauldin

The Value of this Book

Not every military career field makes obvious parallels into civilian life. Understanding your knowledge, skills, and desires when translating your real-life military experience into a commercial career is the primary importance of this book. Whether you are searching for a job or choosing a degree program from an online or traditional university, you will find valuable gems to assist in your decision making and planning.

This book is uniquely suited to help you answer the tough transitional questions and guide you to the best-suited career path for you and your family. Allowing the chapters to guide your transitions studies and following the given advice will provide a multi-dimensional capability through assessments, career mapping and industry insight. This multi-dimensional capability is presented in a logical progression and will require personal review and introspection to build a successful personal transition strategy.

> *"You might be a tanker, if...you giggle when your hunting buddies talk about the awesome stopping power of the .308 Winchester..."*
>
> ~ A Dog Named Sabot

Personal Assessments

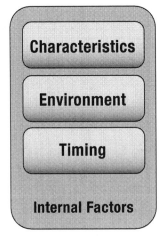

Figure 1.1 | Personal Assessments

A series of personal inventory questions are provided in the areas of environment, characteristics, timing, career field skills, and desired market place options. Some of the factors in the assessments focus upon your internal makeup, while others help organize your desires regarding external variables, as depicted in Figure 1.1.

All assessments aid in creating your strategic roadmap, and help guide you toward a potential career path in a marketable area that you and your family will find satisfying and rewarding. Further, this roadmap provides invaluable insight into your motivations, skill-sets and willingness to seek out the wide variety of opportunities in your next career. Completing the assessments and planning exercises will help you better understand your strengths and weaknesses while increasing your professional skills and personal marketability. The next section provides a detailed look at each chapter and how they will assist in developing your Personal Strategic Roadmap.

Know Yourself *(Chapter 2)*

After thought provoking review of attributes and skills common to many in the military, you will gain an understanding of the importance of your military skills and how they map to major civilian career field groupings (Figure 1.2). This mapping will play an important role in Chapter 3, as we continue to map your skills to commercial occupations.

> *"Total discipline overcomes adversity and physical stamina draws on an inner strength that says 'drive on'."*
>
> ~ SMA William G. Bainbridge

Mapping Chapter 2

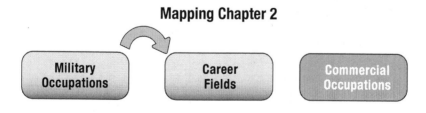

Figure 1.2 | Chapter 2 Mapping Skills to Career Fields

Additionally, you will explore transition timing, lifestyle desires, and personal tolerance for risk. Multiple assessments covering personal and environmental desires are provided. Through these self-assessments, you will gain a documented understanding of your desires as they relate to your transition. Spousal or domestic partner participation in this chapter is recommended; as any transition, just like your previous assignments, determining your future path should be a team decision.

Targeting Your Next Career *(Chapter 3)*

In this chapter, you will gain an understanding of the commercial career fields and their associated occupations, along with the vernacular needed to assist in your transition. From the mapping of your military skills to career fields started in Chapter 2, you will be introduced to various commercial career fields (Figure 1.3). Each commercial career field is further elaborated with associated professions, education and certification. Connecting the dots with this innovative and unique method offered in *The Transitioning Military Series* provides a standardized and no-nonsense approach to translate your military skills into viable, realistic and sensible career opportunities.

Mapping Chapter 3

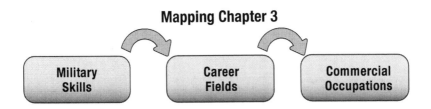

Figure 1.3 | Chapter 3 Mapping Commercial Career Fields and Occupations

You will gain an insider's perspective on career paths, sample job descriptions and corresponding roles/duties. For those wanting to gain that extra edge, we explore different educational degrees, licensure and certifications you can pursue, focusing on applicability and Return on Investment (ROI). A crosswalk of terminology, resources, and the basics of commercial concepts will help you to frame your expectations. Through the skills assessment, your answers give you a realistic view of your potential alignment to various career fields.

The Market Place *(Chapter 4)*

Here we look at three markets for *The Transitioning Combat Arms Professional* after the Service: Department of Defense (DoD) contracting, civil service, and commercial (or corporate) environments. Obviously, there are significant differences between the military and commercial markets. We present many of the different characteristics of the market, outlining pros and

> " *I can't see how a single man could spend his time to better advantage than in the Marines.* "
>
> ~ Sgt. Maj. Daniel Joseph Daly, USMC

cons of each. Entrepreneurship, non-profit, and Federally Funded Research and Development Centers (FFRDC) are discussed briefly. The marketplace assessment helps guide you through a process to assist you in determining your risk tolerance, job creativity, income needs, and stress levels.

The Right Fit *(Chapter 5)*

Assessment results throughout previous chapters are organized and analyzed developing a personal index, unfolding your personal roadmap, and plotting out your best-suited transition. Key indicators from your environmental, characteristics, career field skills, timing, and marketplace assessments become clearly stated courses of action supporting your roadmap. With this information and courses of action in hand, you are given options to pursue for your strategic goals and objectives. Executing your Personal Strategic Roadmap will be key to finding and pursuing the best transition path and job based on your assessment results.

Conventions used in this Book

Each chapter highlights common challenges and provides additional resources for your personal growth. Throughout the book, the star box (shown on the right) is used to call your attention to important facts to further investigate and use for transition. Sources vary from web sites, book references, credentialing materials, or other programs and resources for commercial work and management.

Great information here.

Appendices and Website

Associated with this book is the GR8Transitions4U.com website. This book and website provide a repository of easily accessible resources and experiences to assist you in your transition. Tools, assessments and templates are available in the appendices. Having purchased this book, you are also eligible for the companion guide, where reusable tools and templates are

Free Companion Guide
GR8Transitions4U.com

provided in electronic format online through the GR8Transitions4U.com website. Beyond the confines of these pages, the web site offers periodic updates of materials, statistics, and success stories. These are provided so you can capture and harness the value of this book and its material now and in the future.

Regardless of the path you choose, use this book and the associated assessment tools from each chapter as a system to assist you in compiling your Personal Strategic Roadmap. This will provide a guide and assist the discovery of the most lucrative course of action for your transition.

The only question remaining is: Have you thought of everything you need in order to make the right decision? Let's find out!

Many great stories come from every day people, which often inspire and motivate others. Dewey Tate, is one such story. Dewey's initial experience as a dish washer in college, and later as an Army Artilleryman, enabled his eventual development to a highly-successful business leader.

Dewey Tate
Audacity

TO AN OUTSIDER, DEWEY TATE'S FUTURE WOULD SEEM DISHEARTENING. HE WAS BORN INTO A POOR FAMILY IN THE RED CLAY LANDS OF ALABAMA WHERE LIFE WAS DIFFICULT AT BEST. Fortunately, with a garden plot, 50 acres of farmland, a plow, a mule and a tremendous amount of work, his family produced enough food to sustain themselves.

Dewey's shirts were made from the cloth of feed and flour sacks. Except for two pairs of bib overalls and a new pair of shoes once a year for church, he never had any store-bought clothing. In fact, Dewey went to school barefoot until the third grade.

Wanting a better life, Dewey diligently worked to be admitted to Jacksonville State University in Alabama, where he landed a work scholarship. On top of a heavy full time class load, he washed dishes in the school cafeteria 30 hours per week. Like all able-bodied males, he had to serve in the Reserve Officers' Training Corps (ROTC) program. During his junior and senior years, Dewey was selected for Advanced ROTC and received a paid stipend of 90 cents per day.

Upon graduation, Dewey was commissioned as a second lieutenant in the Army's Field Artillery (FA). With human lives at stake, a zero tolerance for mistakes was mandated. Thus, Army Artillery quickly taught Dewey the importance of attention to detail.

Dewey's first assignment was to Fort Hood, Texas where he served in a Fire Direction Center (FDC) for the Second Armored Division. Due to mounting international tensions, he was deployed to the Fulda Gap in Germany, the primary invasion route from East to West. After returning to Fort Hood, Dewey was deployed back to Germany just a few months later. He quickly found himself in the challenging situation of replacing the Fire Direction Officer (FDO) who was relieved of duty following poor performance in field operations.

Being a newlywed with three deployments in two years, Dewey decided to look for a civilian job. He was determined to move on from the military lifestyle that was causing significant personal challenges.

Having learned the value of people while on active duty in the Army, a friend within his military network had a connection with the chemical manufacturing company, DuPont. Dewey jumped on the employment opportunity.

Moving to the Shenandoah Valley of Virginia with DuPont, his leadership skills landed Dewey a position as a first line supervisor. His military experience enabled him to perform well in his first civilian experience. Subsequently, he was given a challenging job re-writing the Human Resource (HR) manual for the company, a two-inch thick manual of rules, regulations and company benefits. Finishing ahead of schedule, he was given the opportunity to influence his next position within DuPont. He became a supervisor within the Lycra® branch, which was a new and lucrative product being produced by the company. With Dewey's earlier experience, he understood the HR processes and knew how to work with people – critical capabilities for any leader. Dewey had several subsequent promotions and soon had several supervisors working for him.

The U.K. company, Imperial Chemical Industries (ICI), recruited him to come to Richmond, Virginia and assist in *building a new plant that was a significant expansion for the company in the U.S. Dewey solidified his reputation as a good manager who could also control costs on such projects. He credits his Army experience of paying close attention to detail for enabling these capabilities. After six years with ICI, he became an area supervisor of a large plant.*

With this experience, Wabash DataTech in northern Illinois, offered him a management position over multiple plants, with a company aircraft for commuting. It is not hard to imagine Dewey reflecting on his life as he flew between plants in Illinois and Indiana, and visited customers around the country.

A few years later, Gulf Canada, a division of Gulf Oil, offered Dewey an opportunity to come to Atlanta to help build yet another plant in a new location. While the plant was under construction, Dewey and three other associates operated as the corporate officers. Interestingly, Gulf Canada changed their strategy on this plant and offered Dewey and his associates an opportunity to purchase the plant. Taking a huge financial risk, the team incorporated and took out personal loans sufficient enough to acquire the new facility. Soon they were producing synthetic materials for multiple industries and acquired patent rights to a new process that would change history. This new capability for the landfill industry allowed them to build a mountain from layering refuse and dirt on a synthetic grid that Dewey and his associates called "Mount Trashmore." Today, their pioneering work in geo-synthetic materials and geo-grid techniques are performed around the world. At that time, these concepts were revolutionary.

When Islip, New York came under fire by the Environmental Protection Agency (EPA) for dumping garbage into the Atlantic Ocean, a fully-loaded trash barge, owned by the city was forced to cruise up and down the eastern seaboard looking for a port that would allow it to offload the trash. Dewey and his company came to the rescue by assisting Islip with the disposal of their garbage. This situation gave the company national publicity on various television networks. Their efforts were featured on the Discovery Channel and the company was rewarded greatly for their efforts in solving the challenges associated with the disposal of large amounts of urban wastes materials.

Today, Dewey reflects on his poverty as a child and realizes that his military Service to the country, coupled with DuPont's training gave him the experience, maturity and leadership capabilities needed to reach his goals. Dewey believes that his metamorphosis from a shoeless childhood to corporate leader and philanthropist could have occurred "only in America."

Fear of poverty has been Dewey's greatest motivator throughout life. However, he gives the Army full credit for having turned him into a man by giving him tremendous responsibility as a young officer. Further, his military experience made him realize that the key to success is through effectively leading people.

Dewey also credits the Army for teaching him leadership and DuPont for teaching leadership application in the commercial world.

Know Yourself

TO TRANSITION WELL, YOU NEED TO KNOW YOURSELF. A good understanding of your personal traits and characteristics that made you successful in the military is essential. Part of this understanding is an awareness of personal environmental factors to include a keen sense of timing. Knowing yourself and where you are going are the best ways to determine your level of readiness for transition. The more you know about yourself, the easier it is to plan and the better prepared you will be for your transition.

> *"If you know the enemy and know yourself, you need not fear the result of a hundred battles."*
>
> ~ Sun Tzu 孫子
> *The Art of War*

If you do not know what you want to do or where you want to go, you are not alone. Figuring out your future can be daunting. This chapter is an exploration of you, your characteristics, and desires. You will also discover why you are attractive to the commercial sector. To perform this task, Chapter 2 is broken into three major sections.

1. *"Personal Characteristics"* – There are four topics in this critical section. You will first look at method to gain a passion for your transition, job search and work. Afterwards, you will look at your personal characteristics and values. You will then gain an understanding of why your military characteristics are desirable by commercial companies. Later, you will gain an understanding of how your military skills fit into the transitional puzzle.

> *"At the center of your being you have the answer; you know who you are and you know what you want."*
>
> ~ Lao Tzu

2. *"Personal Environmental Factors"* – You face many personal challenges as you transition. This section steps you through many of these factors that can create unwanted challenges.

3. *"Timing Factors"* – There are many preparatory actions that you should consider, all of which may affect your departure time from the Service. In this section, you will consider your transition readiness regarding timing.

To get the most out of this chapter, you will perform a series of assessments. Honest introspection is not an easy task, but doing so will prove valuable throughout these exercises. The more you know about yourself and the more you can plan, the better prepared you will be for transition. All assessments in this chapter provide an introspective look at your internal personal factors. As depicted in Figure 2.1, three critical assessments are offered on the following internal characteristics and desires:

- **A Characteristics Assessment** to gain an understanding of your military skills, and perhaps undiscovered skills that will translate well to a civilian career.

- **An Environmental Assessment** that will challenge your understanding of outside factors such as location, retirement, family, schools and faith. If you are married or have a significant other, it is highly recommended you both take the assessment. Afterwards, discuss any results that might warrant more detailed analysis to offer better alignment.

- **A Timing Assessment** to determine how ready you are to transition based upon the availability of time for planning or need for immediate action.

All assessments will then be incorporated into the development of your Personal Strategic Roadmap, presented in Chapter 5. But, before we start, lets talk about your retirement and future work situation.

Personal Assessments

Characteristics

Environment

Timing

Internal Factors

Figure 2.1 | Chapter 2 Assessments

Retirement

This is a brief note for our retiring readers. You may soon be able to enjoy a military retirement. Military retirement is worth millions over your lifetime. If you retire at 40, you may live another 40 years or more. Not only are you getting roughly 50% or more of your base pay that is adjusted every year or two, you are also receiving medical coverage. The health insurance is a massive savings of hundreds, if not thousands of dollars per month. If you had an annuity that paid this well, it would be worth $500,000 or more with a return of 10% per year to have this kind of income and protection.

If you have saved well and can live within your means, then you may have the tremendous luxury of not having to work. Very few will experience this luxury at such a young age. The real question is whether your military retirement pay is enough to live on for the rest of your life?

For most people retiring from the military Services after 20 years, the answer is most likely "no," as the cash flow is probably not enough for most people to retire immediately.

Even if you could manage financially, after a while you will probably want to find some source of work to keep yourself occupied and productive. Ryan Guina of the Military Wallet states,

The key to being able to retire on your military pension is paying off as many loans and credit cards as possible *before* you officially retire from the military. Debt is the quickest way to enslave yourself and tie up your future pension checks. But eliminating your debt gives you the opportunity to use your money for more important things, such as your regular living expenses, vacations, and other enjoyable activities.[1]

If you are like most and you believe you must or desire to work, then keep reading. The rest of the book is for you.

Occupation or Vocation?

This brief section is a side note for those that have never considered the terms occupation and vocation. One of the many challenges that you will face during transition is the vexing decision of paying bills or pursuing your dreams. You will probably spend considerable time thinking about enabling uninterrupted cash flow, the best company to pursue and what location to settle. Reflection, analysis and alignment of your life's work will be pushed to another day, never enabling full personal passion. As stated earlier, within the graveyard lay all the unwritten novels, un-launched business and all the things that were to be accomplished tomorrow.[2]

The bottom line is that, many of us have yet to discern the difference between our occupation and our vocation. You may not find contentment in your occupational tasks, as you potentially will not be fulfilling your dreams and you may find yourself continually frustration.[3] It takes time and reflection to discern your life's work. "Our occupation is how we make a living… Our vocation, on the other hand, is what we're inherently wired for. It's less likely to consist of a set of tasks and more likely to consist of a set of themes."[4] Tremendous satisfaction is found when making a living while pursuing your life's work. Can you enable this situation as you transition? You will gain more energy and stamina, be happier and more productive if you can incorporate your vocation into the next phase of your life. Understand that if you choose to pursue your vocation, you may have to augment your cash flow by working in an occupation until the vocation begins to pay off. Figure 2.2, displays how these pieces fit together.

Occupation Vs. Vocation

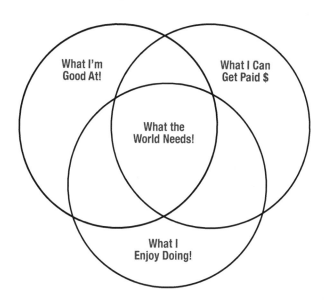

Figure 2.2 | Occupation Vs. Vocation

Remember, your vocation is your life's work. It is what the world needs you to do. It is what you were meant to do--and deep down inside, what you have always wanted to do. So, take time out of your busy transition schedule for introspection and reflect upon your desires and talents. Now, on with the understanding of you.

Who Are You?

As a child, everyone ponders answering the question "When I grow up, I want to be a [___]." When young, it is easy to answer without giving a thought to the consequences. As we get closer in age to the reality of making this choice, we must consider our experiences, knowledge and family evolutions that have made us who we are today. We have to ask "Who am I? What am I good at? What have I done? What do I like to do?" Now you are at a point in time where you are pondering these questions again. So, do you know what you want to be when you grow up? From a job transition standpoint, let's explore your characteristics, core values, and Knowledge, Skills, and Abilities (KSAs) as depicted in Figure 2.3. If you know who you are, what you want and what you can offer, are you able share these personal characteristics through your resume and interviews? Let us review your characteristics and values that are inherently you and then assess your desires.

Who Are You?

Figure 2.3 | Who are You?

Personal Characteristics

What are you made of? Character, derived from the word characteristic, refers to the essence of a person or thing. Character is the combination of traits and attributes that makes us different from one another, as shown in Figure 2.4. More than likely, you've retained many of the same personality traits since birth; examples include being outgoing, reclusive, shy or sociable. Understand your characteristics and how you can use these to add value for your future employer.

Character

Figure 2.4 | Character

Attributes, as opposed to traits, are not ingrained. Attributes are learned over time and are based on external experiences and the behaviors you exhibit. Therefore, as a military Service member, you may have developed strong attributes during a challenging and difficult professional career or situation, such as combat or peace-keeping operations. Attributes such as motivation and enthusiasm are examples that may change during your life or professional experience. A person may be committed to a particular cause or have strong integrity. He or she may be loyal or hard working. These attributes lead to certain behaviors, which can be strong predictors of how one will respond to different stimuli in the work environment.

It is essential to know your traits and attributes as they define your personal characteristics and character. Understanding yourself at this level helps you determine your best career choice. For example, do you enjoy working with other people or prefer working alone? Do you like thinking outside the box? Do you like managing people? Do you perform well under stress? How has the military Service shaped you and your attributes?

Manager or Technician? Indian or Chief?

Your military leadership and management skills will carry you a long way, but there are several questions that you should ponder. One of the first character questions to reflect upon is what type of work you want to do. You will need to decide if being a worker or becoming a manager best suites your personality.

With your skills from the military and your leadership ability, you may find you are well suited for both. However, knowing yourself and your personal desire is essential when making the determination.

This universal question affects nearly everyone and is encountered at some point in time during your career (Figure

"*Leadership doesn't just happen. Leadership is an art. The exercise of leadership connotes dedication, vigor, and endurance- three qualities so essential...*"

~ SMA Silas L. Copeland

23

2.5). Both paths offer benefits and advantages depending on what you desire and what you are good at. Do you like leading and managing teams, resolving conflicts, or offering your expertise? Or do you desire to learn more about a technology or work with your hands to create something tangible.

The Decision

Figure 2.5 | Specialist / Manager Decision

Making the Decision

There are many things to consider when choosing to become a manager. First, know that when choosing the management route, you will be in leadership roles and must rely on a team working for you. Second, there is a misconception that management positions often correlate with better pay. This is not always the case. Management takes a certain mindset and demeanor, as you will need to balance the needs of the executives with those of your peers and within your team or group. Key to commercial management is the ability to communicate well with your audience, using their language. Learning to speak the language of executives will be key as most who are promoted into management bring with them a technical background and expertise. When dealing with other departments, you need to be a mediator and facilitator.

As a team leader, you need to know your team, back them up and earn their trust while removing obstacles for your team members to succeed. Being able to communicate upwards while keeping everyone synchronized and focused are also key elements.

Why do you need to know this? You cannot expect people to jump when you tell them to, as if you were still in the military. This will be a difficult challenge for some. You must understand that many people desire a servant leadership style and have an expectation that you will jump in and provide the help necessary (tools, your time, materials, etc.) to help the organization be successful. They want you to be firm, tough and fair. They do not want you to bark orders, walk away, and have an expectation that that the work will be completed. Remember, there is no civilian Uniform Code of Military Justice (UCMJ) equivalent for disobeying lawful orders in the civilian world.

There are inherent advantages for those going the management route. You will not only gain higher-level organizational and leadership skills, you will also understand the business side of the operation/organization and gain greater potential for climbing the corporate ladder.

Remember, know yourself and move to what you find enjoyable and rewarding, as this is where you will be most successful.

Your Military Attributes

Along with your military skills, employers find the characteristics and attributes gained from your military experience invaluable. From a military perspective, you have led teams and can adapt to different situations rapidly. Additionally, you are educated and tech savvy, a quick learner, possess a security clearance, and perform well under pressure. These attributes make you highly marketable to employers.[5]

In addition to your personal attributes, the military has shaped you with Service-specific core values. People hear the words *Loyalty, Duty, Respect, Selfless Service, Honor, Integrity,* and *Personal Courage* all the time. To you, they are much more than words. Each core value rep-

> " *I want to succeed in the thing I started out to do. I hate failure. I hate quitters.* "
>
> ~ Sergeant Audie Murphy

resents a tremendous personal quality. These values were ingrained during your initial training and endure to this day. You will probably live these values every day in everything you do for the rest of your life. Core values are presented below in Figure 2.6.

Service	Core Values
Army	Loyalty, Duty, Respect, Selfless Service, Honor, Integrity, Personal Courage
Marines	Honor, Courage, Commitment

Figure 2.6 | Service Core Values

In addition to your Service core values, your traditional military skills such as professionalism, leadership, confidence, positive attitude, communications and organizational skills are all highly desired by commercial companies. Forbes recently published the following five key reasons to hire veterans (Figure 2.7).

Quality	Description
Leadership	Platoon leader, group leader, team leader: military veterans work in a highly team-oriented and hierarchical environment. This means they know how to take orders – and when to give them.
Grace under pressure	If you're on the front lines in a war, you need to stay calm and function under extreme pressures. It makes some HR and management calamities look trivial – after all what we do is HR/people management, not ER.
Performance and results-oriented	When you're in uniform you have a mission, one on which lives may be dependent. Performance and results are non-negotiable. You know how to get things done and you do them.
Self-sacrifice	Self-awareness and self-sacrifice. Leaders in the military have to watch out for their teams first and themselves second, which is a leadership scenario not always encountered in the Fortune 500.
Communication and goal-setting	Effective communicators build teams. Leaders set goals and teams accomplish them. You can't have one without the other.

Figure 2.7 | Five Reasons to Hire Veterans[6]

By virtue of military Service, you already know how to track issues on a daily, if not hourly, basis. You have had to reassign tasks to other Service members, take and/or give fitness tests, and oversee weapons cleaning. These organizational qualities are key for any successful professional. It has been said that the difference between success and failure is based on whether you are highly organized or not. Are you?

Other functional skills and experience gained in the military are what will get you in the door for a job interview. Some veterans have experience performing highly marketable functions by being on a battalion staff or working for the commander. Others may have formalized military or commercial training and have spent years in the career field. It is important to translate these skills for the industry and marketplace you desire to move.

> "*Don't let anybody tell you, you are anything less than the cream of society. You should be proud to talk about what you, as a soldier do every day.*"
>
> ~ SMA Kenneth O. Preston

We Want You!

A survey recently published by the Society for Human Resource (HR) Managers provides insight into employers and their thoughts on hiring former military personnel. HR professionals from across many different U.S. based companies and sectors provided the survey data.

On a positive note, companies believe there are many benefits to recruiting and hiring veterans. The most commonly cited quality is a sense of responsibility and ability to see efforts through to completion. In fact, an overwhelming 97% of companies surveyed believe the veteran's strong sense of responsibility is their number one factor in hiring former military Service members.[7] However, some companies have misperceptions about the risks and challenges associated with hiring employees with military experience. For example, the survey demonstrated in some cases a concern that former military employees required additional time to adapt to new workplace cultures. An option for you is to gravitate toward military friendly companies. The good news; there are numerous military friendly companies. Many large corporations such as Google, Chase, Amazon, and FedEx target veterans and provide resources and veteran support programs assistance. By knowing the environment and yourself, you can make quality decisions on potential future employers.

The United States Automobile Association (USAA) hires veterans of all ranks and is one of the most veteran-friendly companies in America today. Many technical companies, such as AT&T and Verizon are among the top 100 military friendly companies. Intel is on this list with over 8% of their employees being veterans. In 2013, 25% of all new hires at Union Pacific Railroad were

ShowyourStripes.org provides a list of the Top 100 Military Friendly Companies for jobs!

veterans. Defense contracting companies, such as L-3, General Dynamics, Booze Allen Hamilton, BAE, CACI, etc., are always looking for military personnel. In fact, almost 25% of all Lockheed Martin employees are veterans.[8] Figure 2.8 lists the top ten military friendly companies for 2016.

2016 Top Ten Military Friendly Companies

1. USAA	6. ManTech International Corporation
2. CSX	7. Southern Company
3. Deloitte	8. Combined Insurance Company of America
4. Booz I Allen IHamilton	9. General Electric Company
5. Burlington Northern Santa Fe	10. J.B. Hunt Transport

Figure 2.8 | 2016 Top Ten Military Friendly Companies[9]

Therefore, you will want to research and understand companies, and speak commercial vernacular to demonstrate your understanding of the job requirements. Understanding the job you are applying for and how the job relates to the company's line of business will provide the opportunity for you to demonstrate knowledge and intellect, validating that you are a fantastic candidate.

Your challenge is to perform introspection and consider yourself and your military skills, the industry, and the associated marketplaces. You must properly align your experiences, skills and interests to determine the opportunities you desire to pursue for your next career. Properly translating this information into a transition strategy will be exciting and critical for your successful jump to the commercial market. Know that your skills and your abilities are desired, you just need to be able to translate them to actual career fields and positions. Let's get started!

Tool for translating your military skills civilian jobs!
military.com/veteran-jobs/skills-translator

Skills Translation

An understanding of how to translate and apply your skills to the commercial sector is vital to your transition. Gaining an understanding of how your leadership skills from your military experience relate to the commercial sector is essential.

To perform this task, let's first identify your developed skills from your Service as a Combat Arms Soldier in the military. Figure 2.9 below presents many skills acquired by most armor, infantry, and artillery soldiers and marines. This figure is obviously not all-inclusive, as many military occupations have some level of technology related skills that are either trained or become an inherent portion of the job. However, this table may provide good input for your "additional skills" section on your resume.[10]

"The leadership stuff you did for years is not going to change, but technology and equipment are."

~SMA Jack Tilley

Resume Skills List For Combat Arms

Leadership Training	Ability to Conform to Rules and Structure
Ability to Work as a Team Member and as a Team Leader	Flexibility and Adaptability
Ability to Get Along with and Work with All Types of People	Self-Direction
Ability to Work Under Pressure and to Meet Deadlines	Educated
Ability to Give and Follow Directions	Initiative
Drug Free	Work Habits
Security Clearances	Standards of Quality and Commitment to Excellence
Systematic Planning and Organization	Global Outlook
Emphasis on Safety	Client and Service-Oriented
Familiarity with Records and Personnel Administration	Specialized Advanced Training

Figure 2.9 | Resume Skills List for Combat Arms[11]

You may be thinking, "I did a lot more than that!" You are correct. Your other functional and technical work performed plays a major role in your transition success. Some transitioning Service members will enjoy some of the aspects of their military occupation such as security training and will be able to apply their skills performing similar work in the commercial sector.

Understanding Your Qualitative Skills (Soft Skills)

The last thing most Combat Arms veterans want to talk about is soft skills. However, when it comes to the job market, there is a tremendous advantage to understanding and articulating the tremendous soft skills that you have obtained during your career. In fact, soft skills are highly-valued and highly-sought-after because they help keep organizations operating effectively.

Soft skills are personal attributes that enable someone to interact effectively and harmoniously with other people. The term soft skills are desirable qualities for employment that do not depend on acquired knowledge that include common sense, the ability to deal with people, and a positive flexible attitude.[12] Believe it or not, this is an area in which you have a definite competitive advantage.[13] Figure 2.10 provides the top 10 soft skills most executives perceive as needed in today's workplace from a study conducted by research analyst, Dr. Marcel Marie Robles.[14]

Top Ten Soft Skills Needed for Today's Workplace

Integrity	Communication
Courtesy	Responsibility
Social Skills	Positive Attitude
Professionalism	Flexibility
Teamwork	Work Ethic

Figure 2.10 | Top Ten "Soft Skills" Needed for Today's Workplace

Skills Translation Tools

There are numerous web sites that offer translators for military skills. These skills translators are very useful for converting your Military Occupational Specialty (MOS) or skills from the military to commercial career fields. However, these translators are generally one-dimensional and single threaded. In Figure 2.11 below, one such on-line translator and job assistance source suggests the following for "Army 11B, Infantryman:"

At first glance, this is a great variety of jobs and locations. All of these are great jobs and may be available to you. In fact, some of these maybe in line with your aspirations. Continuing to serve the nation as a contractor or police officer is a definite route that is available and may provide a significant level of personal pride and accomplishment.

Job	Organization	Location
Range and Training Program Manager, Senior	Booz Allen Hamilton Engineering Services	Guam, US
CIED Trainer	Booz Allen Hamilton Engineering Services	Colorado Springs, CO
Military Intelligence Company (MICO) Trainer	Raytheon	Afghanistan
Sr Training & Develop Spec	Raytheon	Hohenfels, Germany
Military Training Analyst	Raytheon	Afghanistan
Military Medical Trainer (SMW SOAG KAIA)	Raytheon	Afghanistan
Security Guard	G4S	Atlanta, GA
SWAT Team Officer	City of Tampa	Tampa, FL

Figure 2.11 | On-line Job Assist for 11B

However, maybe you are tired of Afghanistan and you no longer consider Hohenfels to be the garden spot of Germany. Further, maybe you no longer desire to have a defense or military-related jobs. Perhaps you do not desire to work as a security guard or police officer. Therefore, you must perform some personal analysis to understand your other great abilities performed and developed while in the military.

Mapping Your Functional Capabilities

Let's look at other functional training and experience that you received while in the Service. You are far more complex with many skills and capabilities to offer a commercial organization. You just need to recognize these qualities and know how to organize them for your resume and the hiring organization.

By way of example, you may have worked with intelligence units or sections in the Army or as a radio chief in the Marine Corps. In doing so, you gained considerable computer or network experience and now desire a career move to the Information Technology (IT) career field as a civilian. However, you may need some certification and training. There are a great many paths you can take.

Your many functional skills are connected to actual career fields and positions. This unique and consolidated method allows for greater ease of understanding the numerous career fields available to you during transition. Later in Chapter

3, we will see how these "other skills" translate to the commercial world, with a description and recommended method for obtaining the various positions through preparation, education, and certifications.

To begin the mapping, you should analyze what functions that you not only performed during your military career, but which of those you also enjoyed. For instance, you may have served on the battalion staff, in the company orderly or supply room. You may have had recruiting duty or served as a trainer at a military schoolhouse. Further, there are numerous additional duties found in each Army and Marine Corps Unit.

As you are aware, the battalion is typically the smallest military organization capable of independent operations. Having worked in, around, and with the battalion structure, most of us will be very familiar with this organization (Figure 2.12). The Battalion Staff provides multiple capabilities to supported units and the commander that include the following primary functions:

> "*Neither a wise nor a brave man lies down on the tracks of history to wait for the train of the future to run over him.*"
>
> ~ Dwight D. Eisenhower

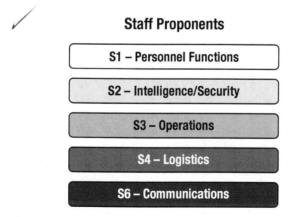

Staff Proponents

- S1 – Personnel Functions
- S2 – Intelligence/Security
- S3 – Operations
- S4 – Logistics
- S6 – Communications

Figure 2.12 | Staff Proponent

Using the battalion staff as a familiar model, Figure 2.13 demonstrates the alignment and integration of the major staff functions. To ease understanding, many of the functions and additional duties that you may have performed align to a staff proponent within the battalion headquarters (HQ).

Take a close look at all the functions listed. There is a good chance that you have been responsible for and/or performed work within many of these areas.

Staff Function Alignment

	Related Functions	Other Additional Duties
S1	Recruiter, Orderly Room Clerk, Medic, Training NCO, Retention	Tax NCO, Class A Agent, Equal Opportunity, Family Readiness, Public Affairs
S2	Orderly Room Clerk, Arms Room NCO	Key Control NCO, Class A Agent, Classified Records Custodian, Security Manager, Phycial Security, Line of Duty, Unit COMSEC
S3	Orderly Room, Ops NCO Training NCO, Recruiter, Reserve Advisor, Platform	Force Protection, Security Manager, Unit COMSEC, Mobilization NCO, QTB, Range NCO / Safety, IG Team
S4	Motor Pool, Supply Room, NBC Room, Armorer, Property Book NCO	Convoy Control, Hazmat Control, Mobilization NCO, IMPAC Card Calibration, Dispatcher
S6	RTO, Informations Systems Security Officer / NCO, Orderly Room	Force Protection, Calibration, Publications, Security Manager, Webmaster, Computer Repair

Figure 2.13 | Staff Function Alignment

Each function and additional duty from the branches of military Service discussed earlier, can be mapped or organized into the major staff proponents. This mapping is generalized and considerations for the mapping are in the next section. Further, if one of your functions or additional duties that you performed is not in the Staff Function Alignment, you will still be able to align your skills and desires to commercial sectors as you continue reading.

Functional Alignment Considerations

It is important to understand this alignment as the staff functions will map to commercial opportunities in Chapter 3. While not a perfect solution, this mapping serves to relate or 'chunk' the majority of the military staff functions into its most basic commercial occupational career field. However, there are a few considerations that could impact and influence the most appropriate career field for you.

1. **Skills transcend many fields.** Many of the functional skills fall into battalion staff proponents. This solution is based on aligning functional tasks to a singular, primary career field to create a starting point for dialog as it relates to transition.

2. **Skills emphasis not formal.** Even though you may have been assigned a position of MOS while in the Service, you may have performed considerable work that is more closely aligned with one of the other functional areas or staff proponents outside of your MOS. This is quite common in headquarters environments where one is expected to perform multiple skills and multiple jobs in the absence of peers or shortages of staff.

3. **Cross training insights.** You may have received considerable cross training or formal training in another career field or staff proponent. This happens often in an environment where new equipment, systems or technology is coming into the organization and you can obtain initial training in this area.

4. **Career desires.** Finally, you may have performed work in a particular MOS or staff function, but may find that you have an affinity or desire to work within a different commercial career. You may have had experience in one or more career fields and enjoyed that experience more than working in the aligned battalion staff proponent. Reflecting on these considerations will offer you a method for assisting in your selection of an appropriate initial post-military career. In turn, this process will improve your focus on how to build your resume, and where to seek employment.

Translation take-away

Regardless of your experience in the Service, your knowledge and management experience will vary greatly by both your individual military career path and assignments. You need to be able to translate this experience into vernacular applicable to and/or universally recognized within the commercial environment you are interested in pursuing. To assist with this translation, further mapping of your military functions to the commercial sector is provided later. Remember, you are unique and you must be able to relay your experiences to the commercial hiring manager.

Assessment #1 *(Personal Characteristics)*

Assessment one, presented in Figure 2.14 challenges you to analyze your personal characteristics, values, traits, and abilities. Read and answer each question. You can also utilize and print the companion guide to this book, available on-line for download at GR8Transitions4U.com. When you are ready to analyze your assessment results, refer to Chapter 5.

1: Personal Characteristics	Strongly Disagree	Disagree	Neither Agree or Disagree	Agree	Strongly Agree
I enjoy working with and being around people.					
I easily apply my skills and referential knowledge when performing tasks.					
I tend to lead tasks when given the opportunity.					
I can perform well in a stressful environment.					
I adapt quickly to changing environments.					
I enjoy being part of a team effort.					
I have the ability to learn concepts quickly.					
I enjoy cross training, solving problems and finding solutions.					
I have thuroughly analyzed the specialist / management decision with regard to my future career path.					
I proactively desire to learn and experience new concepts and trends.					

Figure 2.14 | Personal Characteristics Assessment

Personal Environmental Factors

As you begin your transition, it is important to understand your personal environmental factors. These factors affect you, your family, and your job opportunities. If you are like most, you will work after you transition from the military. If married, you certainly need to take into consideration your family's environmental requirements as you make decisions. Therefore, ensure you work through this section with them. If single, some of the considerations listed here may be relevant to your extended family or future plans.

> *"...success is to be measured not so much by the position that one has reached in life, as by the obstacles which he has had to overcome while trying to succeed."*
>
> ~ Booker T. Washington

Family and Health

As you transition, you need to consider your special family needs. Being close to extended family may constrain your job searching to certain geographic areas. Proximity to airports and hospitals might also require consideration.

There are many family issues to consider during your transition. Does your spouse need or want to work? Can they find jobs at the location you desire? Will he or she require more training or education? Will you or your family need to be near a university or college? Have you studied or discussed sharing your Post 911 G.I. Bill benefits with your family?

A few questions you should consider are:

- Do you have access to medical care or a Veterans Administration hospital?

- Do you understand the impact on you and your family regarding the loss of military benefits?

- Do you know how much risk you and your family are willing to take with your next position?

Work-Life Balance

Another environmental factor to take into consideration as you transition is your Work-Life Balance (WLB). You have worked hard in the military. Part of the assessment process is understanding where you reside on the WLB continuum. When looking for a job you should consider work-life attributes such as the demands that your occupation will require. Are you ready to climb the corporate ladder? You may find a demanding job and make a lot of money, but is that what you want for your retirement job? Occasionally, you can find a job with great WLB and make lots of money. However, if you make $120,000 you should generally expect to put forth a $120,000 effort.

A good WLB makes for better health and happiness. You can work hard and make a lot of money, but inadvertently affect your health and/or family life. Your personal investment in knowledge and experience will allow you to achieve greater expertise, accomplishment, fulfillment, and financial reward. However, it is easy to get caught up in a cycle of hard work and reward. Be cautious, as a successful career must have balance or one will burn out personally, professionally, or both.

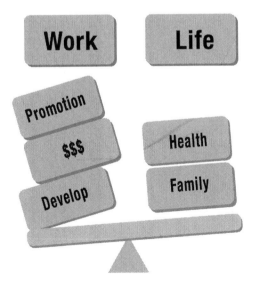

Figure 2.15 | Hazards of Work-Life Balance

Location

Location, Location, Location! - A phrase we are all quite familiar with. A critical consideration is moving to the location of your choice prior to your transition. It can be challenging and very expensive to get back to your U.S. home or to your desired location on your own dime, especially if overseas. You can save a tremendous amount of money if you can have the military move you back to your home of record, or if you can take your last assignment at your desired location. Another advantage to making this happen as part of your transition or retirement would be the ability to begin building your future local network early. If you know where you are going to end up, begin building your network remotely. Here are a few other questions you should ask yourself if you have not already:

10 best places for military to retire:
military.com/military-transition/retirees/10-best-places-for-military-retirees.html

- Have you considered the location of your next job?
- Have you looked at the climate as it relates to your health, hobbies, and personal activities?
- What is the unemployment rate?
- How many government-related jobs exist in the local area?
- What is the cost of living?
- Do you have the need or desire to be near a military base so you can use the commissary, exchange and other facilities?
- Are you looking for a rural or urban life experience?
- Do you wish to live overseas?

Assessment #2 *(Environmental Factors)*

The goal of assessment #2, presented in Figure 2.16, is for you to perform a personal analysis of the associated environmental issues with your transition. As with the first assessment, read each question and choose the best answer. Refer to Chapter 5 when you are ready to analyze the results.

2: Environmental Factors	Strongly Disagree	Disagree	Neither Agree or Disagree	Agree	Strongly Agree
I have performed a post-military financial analysis, to include the loss of military benefits if applicable.					
I have determined my desired geographic location with regard to such factors as healthy lifestyle, allergies, health care access, hobbies, weather and entertainment.					
I have considered my family's special needs in my transition planning.					
I have analyzed and understand myself with regard to work life balance.					
I have given thought to my future location with regard to military base and/or VA Hospital proximity.					
I have studied transition locations with regard to extended family and transportation hub.					
I have analyzed my transition location with regard to future employment, taxation, real estate cost, and overall cost of living.					
I have considered my spouses occupation and their ability to find work.					
I have taken into account my children's primary, secondary and/or college education requirements.					
My family is supportive of my transition into another career.					

Figure 2.16 | Environmental Factors Assessment

Timing

As the saying goes "Timing is everything." As in any transition, timing is a key factor. Are you ready to leave? Do you have to leave? Are you satisfied with your military efforts and ready to move on? These questions are mixed to ascertain your level of readiness to transition from the Service. With regard to your timing, this section includes an analysis of many elements, such as studying the educational benefits, developing and refining your resume, making interview preparations, and approaching certifications. The following timing related topics are presented as rhetorical questions for your comprehension, personal review and self-organization.

Is the Timing Right?

Are you ready to go? You do not want to regret your transition, as there is no going back if you still have something left to do in the military. There are many things to consider about timing. Your gut instinct is probably not the best method for this determination. Looking at the associated timing issues and conducting self-assessments will likely provide you with a better result. These decisions should be made with a clear head and strong conviction. You may not be able to choose when to leave the Service, but you can choose to prepare yourself as completely as possible. The bottom line – prepare the best you can with the limited time you have. Below are some things to consider when deciding if the timing is right to leave the Service.

Are You Having Fun?

This may sound silly, but are you having fun in the military? Only you can determine if you are enjoying your military duty. In general, active duty personnel truly enjoy the military lifestyle and the associated excitement. Many people look back at their time in the Service and remember their experience fondly. Others look back on their military Service as an accumulation of tough days. However, you should expect to have tough days in your civilian job as well. Some will remark, "Wow, did I do the right thing by getting out?" Just remember, the grass is not always greener on the other side of the fence.

Have You Achieved Your Personal Goals for Military Service?

Achieving your personal goals in the military can be quite challenging, especially in today's world. You may have specific goals you were trying to obtain that are no longer attainable. You may also have a brilliant career ahead of you. Making the decision to get out of the Service is always difficult. If you have accomplished your primary goals and objectives for military Service, there is no need to fret about whether you should stay any longer. You may be aware that you have obtained the highest rank possible. Remember, there is a point where you will no longer get selected for promotion. The Congress continually adjusts the size of the military based on the needs of the nation and the defense budget. The Services have had to reduce their end-strengths in the past, are doing so now, and will do so again in the future. During these personnel draw-downs, everyone undergoes assessment and some will be involuntarily released from active duty. If this is your situation, be prepared and transition in a positive manner.

Has A Good Transitional Job Opportunity Presented Itself?

Many veterans have stepped out of the Service straight into great jobs. This occurs with some degree of frequency, but it is not the norm. Often your first job is "transitional." After being out a while, you realize that your first job is probably not the one you truly desire. Remember, it is acceptable to test the waters when you first get out. Regardless, if you desire to grow and develop you may have to move on.

Not everyone will have a job in his or her back pocket when initially transitioning. The question that you should ask yourself is "Am I taking all the appropriate steps for a job opportunity to present itself when ready?"

Are You Prepared to Leave the Service?

Education and Certification

Can you list your skills and education? Are you comfortable with this list? Do you want or feel the need to acquire more? The company that hires you does not always provide skills and education training at the onset. You must be ready to step in and

"When opportunity comes, it's too late to prepare."

~ John Wooden

work. Organizations occasionally offer training; however, you may need to sign an agreement to pay back the training fees or commit to an additional time period. The military is a great environment for training and learning because of all the educational programs and opportunities available. Generally, every branch of Service offers some form of military tuition assistance while on active duty. This lucrative benefit goes away upon transitioning and should be used prior to your departure from the Service. Further, you may be able to get the Service to pay for specialized related certification training before departing. Each Service has on-line guidance for credentialing and certification. Pursue these avenues with a great diligence before departing the Service.

Shortly after your transition from the Service, you should obtain a Post 911 G.I. Bill certificate of eligibility from the Veteran's Administration. This is the

Post 9/11 GI Bill
benefits.va.gov/gibill/
post911_gibill.asp

essential starting point for using this tremendous educational benefit for you and perhaps your family's education. You may be eligible for this VA-administered program, if you have at least 90 days of aggregate active duty Service after September 10, 2001, and are honorably discharged or were discharged with a service-connected disability.[15]

How is Your Financial Readiness?

Have you saved enough money to survive the transition period? These dollars need to be in short-term savings and not locked up in a retirement account in order to avoid tax-related penalties. For many, the question is, "How much should you keep in a 'rainy-day' fund?" According to the Bureau of Labor Statistics (BLS), an acceptable measure of three to six months' worth of expenses may no longer apply. "A lot of experts now recommend that everyone keeps nine months to one year of income in an emergency account in case of job loss," says Gail Cunningham, spokeswoman for the National Foundation for Credit Counseling in Washington, D.C. [16]

Have You Prepared Your Resume?

There is a tremendous amount of information available to assist military veterans in the preparation of their resumes. This book is not intended to be a definitive guide on resume building. However, this guide provides discussions on enhancing the communication of your brand and methods of avoiding common resume "landmines" or pitfalls frequently encountered by your fellow Service members.

> *"Whoever said the pen is mightier than the sword obviously never encountered automatic weapons"*
>
> ~ General Douglas MacArthur

Remember, a powerful, impactful, well-written resume using commercial and business language, combined with the right format and branding power, can set you apart and propel you to a rewarding position in the private sector. Your resume and cover letters are your personal calling cards.[17] To create a well branded and powerful resume you will need to go beyond providing your job description.

Be aware that commercial and civil service resumes can be very different. A few years ago, it was best practice to create a special resume with a specific format when applying for civil service positions. However, with the development of USAJOBS.gov, you can now upload your resume to this website and no longer use a resume builder for civil service jobs.

Your Military Experience is Unique!

Many transitioning Service members have challenges talking about the uniqueness of their military experience with the hiring managers. You must capitalize on the extraordinary capabilities that you have achieved while in the Service. You will need to speak to the value and difference you made while serving in each position.

Need resume assistance:
CorporateGray.com

Capture the size, quantity of personnel, and if applicable the multiple geographic locations that you had to coordinate with and/or synchronize associated with each position. You will need to talk about the impact and volume of what you routinely handled.

Resume Writing: Art and Science

There is a definite skill to writing a resume. It is an art to speak about yourself and connect your value to the value desired by a company. It is a science to include the key terms in your resume so a computerized search engine can identify those words within your resume and put it at the top of their pile for consideration. There are many tools and books to assist you with this.

> *"Be Bold. Most of us have a sense of humility, but a resume isn't the place for it."*
>
> ~ Anonymous

You will most likely need to write and re-write your resume multiple times. Be smart with your network; use military friends and colleagues who have transitioned well for a civil servant position. Use other networking groups from professional or other non-military organizations for commercial insight and guidance. You will need to modify the resume until you are comfortable with it. If you are challenged with resume writing and have money for professional preparation, this may be a good investment.

It is recommended to post your resume on hiring sites like Monster.com, Indeed.com, and CareerBuilder.com. These sites are scanned on a regular basis and you will get frequent emails informing you of potential opportunities. Even if the job is not exactly what you desire, apply! In addition to potentially gaining a greater appreciation for the company and associated career opportunities, the interview experience is very valuable.

Resume Format

Impact! When your resume gets in front of a recruiter or hiring manager, it has approximately twelve seconds to do its job. It needs to be clear and error-free and most importantly, show your value! The three major formats presenting their values are listed in Figure 2.17, below:

Resume Type	Description
Chronological	Starts by listing your work history, with the most recent position listed first. Jobs are listed in reverse chronological order – with current, or most recent job, first. Employers typically prefer chronological, easy to see jobs held and when worked. Works well for job seekers with strong, solid work history.
Functional	Focuses on your skills and experience, rather than on your chronological work history. Used most often for changing careers or gaps in employment history.
Combination (Hybrid)	Lists skills and experience first. Employment history is listed next. Highlights relevant skills to the job you are applying for, while providing chronological work history that employers prefer.

Figure 2.17 - Resume Types[18]

Employers tend to favor a resume that is easy to follow and clearly communicates your professional track. If you plan on writing your own and have 10 or more years of experience and education, select a format that concentrates on your assignments, your accomplish-

Resume Formats:
jobsearch.about.com/od/
resumes/p/resumetypes

ments (value), and education. A great guide for specific resume examples and templates can be found in *"The Military to Civilian Transition Guide: Secrets to Finding Great Jobs and Employers."*[19]

Common Resume Pitfalls

The following errors in resume writing are often found in Service member resumes as they prepare for transition. Avoiding these problem areas will increase the probability of your resume getting through the HR staff screening and into the hands of the hiring official.

Service Member Jargon

There is no place for military jargon or vernacular in your civilian resume. Terms such as command and control, tactics, ISR, execution of battle plans, OPTEMPO, and weaponry mean nothing to a civilian recruiter and are insignificant. This is also true for unit names or assignment locations. Write your resume with the target audience in mind. Most of the people scanning it are HR professionals who understand their industry and recruiting, not mortar ranges and targeting of terrorist networks. Focus on plain business language and your potential value to an employer. Remember, many years of military Service and the word "retired" may arouse undesirable assumptions.

Very Long Resume

A resume should be two pages or less in length. Do not try to cram 25+ years of military Service into the resume. Instead, adjust your format and focus on your last 10-12 years. Employers will thank for you for this.

> *"Be so good they can't ignore you."*
>
> ~ Steve Martin

Resume with No Direction

"Operations manager, sales manager, director of business planning and jack-of-all-trades." Do not let your resume display uncertainty or ambiguous career goals. Your resume should not float between work experience narratives with no central focus. You need to make a decision and decide what you want to place in your objective statement and write your resume to that. You can always change your mind with the next version of your resume or have multiple resumes, but you should focus on one career direction per resume. Remember, you are telling a story and creating a brand for yourself. Your resume must show direction and tell your personal story as it relates to the position for which you are applying.

Job Duties Only

Often a Service member's first cut on a resume focuses on the job duties performed. This makes sense as these are easily transferred from your military evaluations. However this technique does not work. Remember, you are your own best salesman! You need to focus on achievements and the impact you made to show value and worth to your potential employer. By only listing job duties, you are telling a prospective employer you do not bring much to the table other than following directions. If you lack documentable educational degrees, make sure to highlight your professional development training and associated certifications.

Your resume needs to show how you can help provide value from the company's perspective in areas such as financial goals, strategy, market penetration, or process improvement. Demonstrate you are more than an employee and that you are an asset to any team. Believe it or not, everyone else competing for that same job knows this secret!

Getting to the Top

How do you stand out? Getting your resume to the top of a hiring managers list among hundreds of candidates will be challenging. You obviously want your resume to be noteworthy, but you do not want to look arrogant or inexperienced. You must be understood by hiring managers, which can be a difficult task for anyone in transition. Here are a few pointers:

Customize for the Intended Audience

As you transition, you must be flexible and versatile. Make sure your resume is appropriate, as every company and position is different. Therefore, you may need several different versions of your resume; each emphasizing different facets of your career objectives and achievements. Be consistent and do not contradict yourself.

Get to the Point

Consider integrating the specific job posting title into your objective statement. Do not present a high level, generalized and vague comment about how you are looking for a challenging position with a dynamic company as an accomplished professional. Describe your pertinent experiences and qualifications in quick and energetic terms.

Don't Over Embellish, but Tell a Great Story

Recruiters expect a resume to reflect an element of spin, but over exaggeration is detrimental. Shine the most favorable light on yourself and your achievements. However, excessive embellishments may keep you from getting hired. If hired, you run the risk of being placed in a position where you are underqualified and cannot perform well.

Integrate Keywords from the Job Posting

Today, keyword search is a screening criterion. Do not overdo it, but ensure keywords are present in your resume. This is critical for all online applications and resumes as most are screened by computer search engines. Further, you may receive subsequent contacts for positions that you have not applied for. Do you satisfy the criteria on the job posting? If so, do you reflect that on your resume? Get the keywords on your resume.

Avoid "en vogue" Terms and Words

Your resume should not read as if has been pulled from the latest business magazine or thesaurus. Forget over-used words and phrases; try to be original. However, do not overuse big words when simplistic language will do.

Remember, there is no Jedi mind trick to influence your selection by a HR recruiter. Sending out resumes is a matter of trial and error. You must keep submitting and experimenting with different formats and approaches until something works for you. With ingenuity and realistic expectations, you will create a bulletproof resume that represents well and lands you a great job.[20]

Professional Branding

You are a professional brand. You might not necessarily realize this fact when you begin your transition, but it is true. Your resume, LinkedIn® profile, and job applications should all mutually support your common brand. Focus on key items like leadership or a subject matter expertise. Build a brand foundation that resonates throughout the resume. It is important to ensure your professional experience and education reflects who you are. Prospective hiring officials should have no doubt on your level of expertise and what you bring to the table. Make sure your Facebook and LinkedIn pages are strictly professional and synchronized, as hiring professionals look at them.

Achievements

Focus on both your achievements and career history, while highlighting your measurable capabilities and impact on the organization by personifying and enhancing your professional brand. A two-page resume should contain enough power when written well. You must show the impact you made on all previous positions. Listing that you had a job without any impact is wasting valuable resume space. Remember, they are hiring you and what you can bring to the table.

Cover Letter – Icing on the Cake

Experts in the placement field say that the well-written cover letter... not the resume... will land more job interviews. As a transitioning Service member, it is a tragic mistake not to spend the time and effort necessary for a personalized cover letter, each time you submit an application. So, the question is can you rapidly construct a great cover letter? Here is some advice for constructing a great cover letter.

Be Brief

A short, pithy, excited and to the point cover letter will get your cover letter read. HR and hiring managers are not going to read through a long boring document, when they are quickly scanning for the right candidate. Often, less is more.

Layout

Remember to address your cover letter to someone! Find out who will receive the cover letter and address your cover letter to them. If you cannot get this information, open with a subject line like: "Cover Letter: Your Name, Your Credential." Remember, open the cover letter with a hook. The first sentence must grip the reader and will almost guarantee your cover letter and resume get a much closer look. You can do this through one of several methods.

- **Excitement** - You can express your excitement for the job opportunity. This translates to motivation and dedication. This can make HR want to find out more about your qualifications.

- **Using Keywords** - Knowing that scanning or applicant tracking systems are widely used, another approach to the opening line is to make it key-word-heavy.

- **Name Dropping** - Using a connection is a foreign concept to many Service members, because we don't do this in the military. If someone in your professional network refers you, don't hesitate to drop the name, straight away. This is frequent occurrence in the commercial world and people often receive referral bonus for doing so. Remember, time is money and this method helps HR rapidly fill positions with quality candidates.

- **Current Event** – Your cover letter opener can impact employers by demonstrating your knowledge of recent news associated with the company and relate that to the position you are applying for. Let them know why you would be the best candidate as relative to this news.

Make sure your cover letter communicates what you can do for the business, how you will benefit the company and its bottom line. You may need to take a few minutes and perform some internet searches to relate your added value in clear terms.

Ensure you have an enthusiastic ending and request something. Ask the employer for action. Go ahead and request an opportunity to interview this week or at their earliest convenience. Thank them for the opportunity. Your closing should assume you are going to land the interview.

T&T - Transportable & Tailorable

You want to be able to modify and reuse your cover letter repeatedly. So, you need to create a digital folder for cover letters. You need to be able to quickly tailor the opening and letter body to relate your skills to the essential elements of each job announcement. Don't forget to save your cover letter each time for quick modification and future use.

The cover letter is your marketing sheet; its primary purpose being to get job interviews. The more interviews you attend, the wider range of opportunities you will receive. Remember, applying and interviewing for jobs is a career-long process and it takes lots of practice.

Got Interviews?

Practicing interviewing is essential. Interviewing is like fishing – you need to practice. If a resume is your bait and hook, use the interview to reel them in. Seek out and go on interviews regularly just to stay in practice. Interviewing is a very special skill. It takes time and practice to hone your responses to the questions that your future employer will likely ask. Additionally, always be prepared to ask the hiring supervisor questions as well. This is a good indicator that you have done your homework and are showing an interest in what they do. Ensure you have studied the position description before the interview, so you can ask clarifying questions and gain more insight. Be honest during the interview. Do not overstate your capabilities. If you find you are not selected, you can and should ask why. If you make a mistake, you want to know so you can keep from making the same mistake again. Remember the adage: practice makes perfect. You can also inquire about other opportunities they know of within or outside their unit.

> *"I AM ... two of the most powerful words. For what you put after them shapes your reality."*
>
> ~ Anonymous

Can You Communicate Your Characteristics to the Hiring Manager?

Communication is critical when dealing with a hiring manager. Normally, you will only get a few minutes with them. Most will sum up an applicant within the first five minutes. This is the opportunity to tell them what is not on the resume. Let them know you are the best candidate for the job. Huge dividends will be paid to the candidate who, prior to the interview, learns many details about the company and its operations, their future supervisor, and the hiring manager.

After you have written your resume and find yourself in an interview, make sure you approach it with enthusiasm. Interlace discussions of your skills, flexibility, military traits, passion and trustworthiness to the hiring manager. Use personal experiences that resulted in positive end-states. Always communicate your best

"Crafting an Elevator Speech"
mindtools.com

characteristics reflecting the attributes you have. It is time to unfold your story with enthusiasm and relevance to the company. Hiring managers view this positively.

Finally, unless specifically asked, never speak about your shortfalls. However, be prepared to answer the question, "Tell us about a time you failed." These are great opportunities to explain challenges that you have experienced. It is not about the change or failure that happened, it is how and what you did after to carry on and learn from it. What is important is to show how you turned the situation around for the good and future results. You need a great answer in your hip pocket that indicates you learned from the experience.

Have You Developed a Network?

Developing your network is a two-pronged attack. One must have a local network and an internet network. A great way to develop local networks is to volunteer at your local military association such as the Navy League, Association of the United States Army (AUSA), or Armed Forces Communications and Electronics Association (AFCEA). However, getting off the installation and meeting with local organizations is a better way to expand your network. Find your closest Toastmasters Club. By way of example, the Tampa Bay Area has over 51 Toastmasters Clubs. The Project Management Institute (PMI) has chapters in over 110 cities in the United States and 237 chapters around the world. Additionally, there are numerous other professional organizations that you can get involved with around the country and potentially in your local area. Get started with the sampling of networking organizations presented in Figure 2.18 below. These organizations and associations will not only offer national meetings, but often conduct regional and local chapter meetings. Each one of these groups actively seeks volunteers. Volunteer and you will not only grow in your understanding of the commercial professions and enhance professional skills; you will also actively increase your network. Some of these organizations offer certifications, which will be discussed more in Chapter 3.

PMI is one of these professional networking organizations that promotes the professional development of Project Management Professionals in the commercial environment. PMI supports the profession by providing a community of practice where members network and improve their professional skills. PMI seeks to advance the project management profession through standardization and professional development with support of education and advocacy.

Just as important as developing a local network is developing your virtual network. On-line professional networking companies such as LinkedIn® are invaluable. Keeping in contact with friends and acquaintances through LinkedIn® is easy. Social media outlets are a great way to receive the latest news and opportunities. Further, members keep their addresses updated so there is no need to update your address book. This is a perfect method for keeping up with your professional acquaintances. If you have not done so already, build a LinkedIn® account and start building your online network as soon as possible.

"Find local Toastmasters"
Toastmasters.org

EverNote® is another great application that works with your smart phone and LinkedIn®. Simply snap a photo of the business cards you collect from con

Organization	URL
Air Transport Association of America	www.airlines.org
American Economic Association – AEA	www.vanderbilt.edu/AEA/index.htm
American Society of Transportation & Logistics, Inc. – ASTL	www.astl.org
American Trucking Associations, Inc. – ATA	www.truckline.com
APICS - supply chain and operations management	www.apics.org
Association for Computing Machinery (ACM)	www.acm.org
Association for Data Center Management (AFCOM)	www.afcom.com
Association of American Railroads	www.aar.org
Association of Information Technology Professionals (AITP)	www.aitp.org
Association of Shareware Professionals (ASP)	www.asp-software.org
Association of Legal Administrators	www.alanet.org
BDPA (Black Data Processing Associates)	www.bdpa.org
Computer Professionals for Social Responsibility (CPSR)	www.cpsr.org
Council of Supply Chain Management Professionals	www.cscmp.org
Council of Supply Chain Management Professionals – CSCMP	www.cscmp.org
Delta Nu Alpha	www.deltanualpha.org
Eno Transportation Foundation, Inc.	www.enotrans.com
Independent Computer Consultants Association (ICCA)	www.icca.org
Inland Rivers, Ports & Terminals, Inc.	www.irtp.net
Institute for Supply Management – ISM	www.ism.ws
Institute of Electrical and Electronics Engineers (IEEE) Computer Society	www.computer.org
Intermodal Association of North America – IANA	www.intermodal.org
International Association of Public Health Logisticians (IAPHL)	www.IAPHL.org
International Society of Logistics – SOLE	www.sole.org
Material Handling Industry of America	www.mhia.org
National Association of Programmers	www.napusa.org
National Defense Transportation Association - NDTA	www.ndtahq.com
National Human Resources Association	www.humanresources.org
Network Professional Association (NPA)	www.npanet.org
Society for Technical Communication (STC)	www.stc.org
Society for Human Resource Management	(SHRM) www.shrm.org
Software Development Forum (SDF)	www.sdforum.org
The Academy of International Business	www.aib.msu.edu
The Academy of Management	www.aomonline.com
The International Air Cargo Association	www.tiaca.org
The National Industrial Transportation League - NITL	www.ntil.org
Transportation Intermediaries Association – TIA	www.tianet.org
Transportation Research Board TRB	www.trb.org
Warehouse Education and Research Council	www.werc.org
Washington Alliance of Technology Workers (WashTech)	www.washtech.org

Figure 2.18 | Professional Organizations and Associations

tacts and it automatically feeds your LinkedIn® Account. It is a great concept as more and more folks join LinkedIn®. The bottom line is that you need to network. It will pay huge dividends as you depart the Service. Remember to start early.

Transition Assistance Program

Finally, have you attended your local transition assistance program? These programs are essential for teaching you the basics needed for a successful transition. Transition information and counseling for pre-separation, employment assistance, relocation, education and training, health and life insurance, finances, reserve affiliation, disabled veterans, and retirement are provided. However, do not expect to find a job from this program.

> *"The population of earth has reached 7 billion people, every single one of whom send you irritating emails to join something called 'LinkedIn'"*
>
> ~ Dave Barry

SWOT Analysis

As another tool for your transition preparation and ability to know yourself, the Strength, Weaknesses, Opportunities and Threats (SWOT) analysis is presented. The SWOT analysis was originally developed for strategy and marketing and is used extensively by business developers. SWOT is a method for determining competitive advantage in the market place. Use this tool to help determine your competitive advantage to the job market competition. Performing a self-analysis to determine your abilities or challenges within these four areas will not only give you a greater understanding of yourself, but will also provide a level of confidence needed to be competitive. Figure 2.19 below depicts those characteristics or attributes common to military personnel based on their typical military experience.

Strengths	Weaknesses
Internal, positive aspects under your control to exploit:	Negative aspects you control and can improve upon:
Military work experience (Ch. 2)	Lack of commercial work experience (Ch. 3)
Education (Ch. 3)	Lack of understanding of job market (Ch. 3)
Technical knowledge (Ch. 2)	Lack of commercial vernacular (Ch. 3)
Transferable characteristics - communication, leadership, teamwork (Ch. 2)	Negative self-image (Ch. 2)
Personal attributes - ability to work under pressure, work ethic, etc. (Ch. 2)	Dealing with negative misconceptions about military service members (Ch. 2)
Innate Military Core Values (Ch. 2)	Not understanding how to become marketable (Ch. 3)
Ability to assess and perform introspection on your capabilities (Ch. 5)	Lack of commercial experience or career knowledge (Ch. 3)
Ability to gain certification (Ch. 3)	
Opportunities	**Threats**
Positive, external conditions outside of your control that you can exploit:	Negative, external conditions you cannot control, but can reduce the effect:
Career field growth (Ch. 1)	Knowing your competition (Ch. 3)
Military friendly companies (Ch. 1)	Negative misconceptions about former military (Ch. 2)
Opportunities available through further educational and certification (Ch. 3)	Competitors with better job hunting capabilities (Ch. 2)
Funding of school through GI Bill program (Ch. 3 & 4)	Obstacles - lack of education and/or certification (Ch. 3)
Fields in need of military attributes (Ch. 2)	Competitors with superior skills (Ch. 3)
Opportunities available with greater preparation and self-knowledge (Ch. 3)	Failure to stay marketable (Ch. 3)
Opportunities by greater understanding of commercial career field and market place (Ch. 4)	
Networking with seasoned Professionals (Ch. 3)	

Figure 2.19 | Timing Assessment

Assessment #3 *(Timing)*

In assessment #3 (shown in Figure 2.20), you will look at personal preparedness and timing of your transition. As before, read each question and choose the best answer.

3: Timing	Strongly Disagree	Disagree	Neither Agree or Disagree	Agree	Strongly Agree
I I am ready to leave the military experience behind.					
I have met my career goals for the military.					
I am enjoying or looking forward to making plans for my military transition.					
My resume has been completed and reviewed by a civilian professional.					
I have established a network of professionals in and out of the service.					
I have saved several months salary for financial sustainment during transition.					
I have successfully attended a local military transition assistance program.					
I have successfully branded myself on LinkedIn, Facebook or with appropriate professional associations.					
I have practiced my interviewing skills.					
I have performed a personal SWOT analysis.					

Figure 2.20 | Timing Assessment

Knowing yourself is critical when competing in today's job market. Seek professional enhancement at every turn. Do not be afraid to reach out to new opportunities and analyze alternative paths. Try different angles and exploit those areas where you get traction. Above all keep moving forward, no matter the challenge. The story below depicts a former soldier who was resilient in the face of adversity in combat and civilian job market.

Sean Bode –
Everyone Falls, the Strong Get Up

GROWING UP IN NEW ORLEANS, SEAN ADOPTED AN ATTITUDE OF TAKING CARE OF HIS BUDDIES EARLY ON. He often served as the designated driver, to ensure everyone got home safe after having a good time. Working hard during high school in the sporting and academic arenas, Sean secured a position as a cadet at West Point. Shortly after 9/11/01, Sean visited Ground Zero. While rooted in a patriotic instinct, it was a poorly executed decision. Through misrepresenting that he would stay within walking distance to the base and instead traveling 60 miles to NYC, Sean violated both his weekend travel pass and the honor code. Thus, Sean was forced to leave the Military Academy. Sean fully owned his mistake, and during his exit interview told the three-star general superintendent of West Point, that his desire to serve was unshaken and he would earn a commission someday.

As he picked himself up and evaluated his next steps, Sean moved in with his mother in her new home town of Norfolk, Virginia to attend Old Dominion University. In just a few months Sean would recalibrate his direction, staying true to the mission of serving, and found a strong ROTC program at the University of Richmond. While losing a full scholarship initially presented a challenge to bounce back from, Sean realized that by joining the simultaneous membership program with the Army Reserves and working part time, he could fund his undergraduate education. The drive did not come from a desire to join the Service and use sexy equipment like jets or helicopters, instead Sean wanted to be where the soldiers were. Leading, developing, and caring for fellow soldiers inspired Sean to pursue his Bachelor's Degree in Leadership.

Sean commissioned into active duty with his first branch choice as an infantry officer. Starting his career at Fort Benning, Georgia with just a pair of airborne wings and a fire to learn, Sean completed the Infantry Officer Basic Course (IOBC) as an honor grad. Like his professional career, Sean's personal life was improving as he married his college sweetheart, Sarah, and they received orders for their first duty station in Germany. The path became bumpy when an appendectomy derailed his training. Hungry to join his unit, Sean attended Ranger School before he fully recovered and failed to earn his Ranger tab. Once again, Sean could have been down and out; however, he learned the importance of proper preparation and tactical patience from the difficult situation.

Back up and running, the next step was linking up with the Second Striker Calvary Regiment in Vilseck, Germany. After a year of preparing for deployment to Iraq in his first position in the S3 shop, Sean assumed the role of a Platoon Leader. Unfortunately, very little time remained for preparation with the platoon, but Sean recognized the importance of using that time to reinforce their ability to bounce back and adapt to whatever situation arose as a team.

After arriving in Baghdad, Sean's platoon found themselves a few miles south of the green zone, on forward operating base Falcon. Just four months into the deployment, Sean endured another major setback. The platoon was securing a highway intersection when a tragic car accident occurred between the lead Striker vehicle and that of a significant local politician, who was killed. Shortly thereafter Sean was told his talents were no longer needed leading the platoon, but instead was moved to the Squadron S2 shop. Sean was once again devastated. But having learned resilience, he picked himself up and performed the 12-hour night shift to the best of his ability. He subsequently received an opportunity as the headquarters platoon leader with another company. To relieve pressure on the operational tempo of the line platoons, he was asked to train the cooks, fire support, mortar men and snipers into a cohesive unit with patrolling capability. While out on patrol, the platoon engaged in several firefights and Sean's vehicle was hit with an IED. Despite these encounters, Sean is proud all his men came home physically unharmed.

Leaving a five-month-old son and coming home to a twenty-month-old, Sean realized the constant deployments were not the way he wanted to raise a family and decided it was time to move on. Soon after returning to Germany from Iraq, Sean began preparation for transitioning from the Service.

Sean partnered with an organization with a great reputation, but quickly realized the challenge associated with recruiting organizations. Some recruiters have critical jobs to fill so they can continue to maximize profits from placement fees. They plug the right people with the right skills into the right positions, but often do not take into consideration the individual's passions. The recruiter found a job for Sean, but his first commercial work experience was not a pleasant environment. His section was having 100% turnover every year. He knew the culture was not right, but he was determined to stick it out. At first, Sean saw the situation as a challenge to overcome, but over time realized that the company focused on the bottom line at the expense of the employees. Seeking career development and a method for self-improvement, Sean enrolled in Duke's Executive MBA program. After completing about 50% of the program, his vice president changed the company's stance from support and instead encouraged him to stop the degree pursuit as "none of the vice presidents needed an MBA." When Sean refused to quit the program, the VP responded "then you don't need to work here anymore" and let him go. Sean spent time preparing to leave the Army, but he was not ready for the dismissal from his first corporate job.

Once again, Sean was down but not out. Sean rationalized the dismissal as a great gift. It was the push he needed to move forward to a better career, a profession. Staying focused on the mission of joining an organization that took care of their employees and made an impact on the world kept his morale up. By focusing on school, networking with others in respected organizations, and spending quality time with his wife and sons, Sean surrounded himself with a tribe that had his back and supported his success.

After numerous months of networking and preparation, Sean attended a hiring event with Walt Disney World in Orlando, Florida, in conjunction with the Hiring Our Heroes Program, a nationwide initiative to help veterans, transitioning Service members, and military spouses find meaningful employment opportunities. Landing a fantastic job as a HR business partner, he found himself working in an environment where he could share his passion for building teams, developing leaders, and creating a culture of excellence. Never having desired to work in HR, he quickly found enjoyment performing internal consulting, focusing on human capital and providing advice for senior executives. Once again in a healthy organization he could look out for the organization and the "troops."

Sean Bode states that stumbling and even falling down is a part of life. However, those missteps do not have to be career ending. When you fail, by shifting from a victim mindset of "Why is this happening to me?" to a growth mindset of "What am I supposed to learn from this?" you *can get up and keep going. He shares that "many transitioning Service members are either running away from something about the military or running toward something they believe exists outside of the Service. Being crystal clear on your personal mission and what you are running to is key." The Army taught Sean to take responsibility for his actions; to learn and to move on, becoming a stronger and a better person. His advice for long-term career success is to look for the right company, community and mentors that are going to support you.*

Pursuing his passion to support veterans and companies that see the value in employing vets, Sean created Veteran's Journey. An organization dedicated to supporting veterans on their journey to find their mission, tribe, and guide; Veteran's Journey also guides companies on their journey to fully engage the unique skill sets veterans bring to the table to drive organizational growth.

3

Targeting Your Next Career

AN UNDERSTANDING OF HOW TO TRANSLATE AND APPLY YOUR SKILLS TO THE CIVILIAN JOB MARKET IS VITAL TO YOUR TRANSITION SUCCESS. You may perceive you have little e experience of value to the commercial market. However, this could not be farther from the truth. In the last chapter, you gained an understanding of the importance of your personal characteristics, your soft skills, and your values which will assist the enabling of a lucrative and well-fitting post-military position. In this chapter, we are going to take a deeper dive into your military experience and desires and find out how these align to the job market.

The purpose of this chapter is to enhance your understanding of alignment to the commercial job market and enhancing your competitive advantage for transition. An exploration of career fields, down to the job title and related certification level is provided. You will increase personal awareness of commercial opportunities along with some associated terminology and key commercial concepts. Opportunities

> *"Luck is what happens when preparation meets opportunity"*
>
> ~ Roman Philosopher Seneca

will reveal themselves when you become more acquainted with the numerous professions available, as you step through this chapter.

There are three major sections in this chapter:

1. *"The Hunt"* – This background section provides a brief look at the psyche required for the job hunt.

2. *"Certifications and Education"* – This section looks at the logic behind gaining education and/or certification. Pros and cons, and some helpful methods are presented.

3. *"Career Field Details"* – First, utilizing the five staff functions discussed in Chapter 2, this section will map each function to a commercial career field you find desirable. Each career field will offer a commercial overview and list common occupations with general descriptions. Finally, thoughts on gaining appropriate education or certification are discussed for career fields within occupations along with sources for additional study.

Later in this chapter there is a skills assessment, which will determine your potential readiness for transition based on your desires, and KSAs. This assessment will highlight your strengths along with your potential personal development and growth areas. All assessments will then be incorporated into the development of your Personal Strategic Roadmap, presented in Chapter 5.

The Hunt

Getting your game face on for the job hunt is not difficult, but you should know what to do. There are several areas that you need to consider and potentially change or develop.

No doubt, your Combat Arms military experience has hardened you for the emotions of the transitional job hunt, but there are land mines and obstacles on the path. You want to avoid these if possible. Let's look at a few of these.

"They have us surrounded. Those poor bastards!"

~ General Creighton Abrams

Increase Your Self-confidence

Self-confidence and esteem can be lacking in some that are during transitioning, especially if you have been at it for a while. But there is no need for a lack of self-confidence. Do not be concerned that you are military. Remember, you have a great many desirable attributes. Further, you do not have to be a perfect fit, or look and think like the prospective company's typical hire to make a strong impression. Bringing a fresh perspective can give you a competitive advantage. Your originality and differences will often pave the way for innovation. Many employers, especially military friendly employers, will embrace these attributes.

Become a Fanatic

Once you know what career field and occupation you want to pursue, make sure you are familiar with industry and its jargon. This will show employers that you know what you are talking about. Watching for and reading all the news in your selected career field can give you great edge and talking points. Read about your target company and you will come to the interview prepared for their office culture, latest projects and position in their industry. Follow the company on social media to get a better understanding of work life within the organization.

Get Organized

Create your spreadsheets, Evernote lists, 3X5 cards and calendar reminders. Work diligently to keep all of the companies and your research information organized. It is a well-known fact that a cluttered, messy workspace can decrease your productivity. You never know when the phone will ring and you will need to put your hands on critical elements of information.

> "Life is tough. It's even tougher when you're stupid!"
>
> ~ John Wayne

Understand Geographic Employment Trends

Depending on who you ask, the United States job market is either moving forward at an incredible clip or it is still floundering. Regardless of your thoughts on this subject, you should consider the path of least resistance for your transition regarding location. To do this, there are many employment trends and factors to consider concerning locality. Some cities are enjoying a much faster growth rate than others, while still other cities are recessed. According to WalletHub,

Best Cities to Find a job: wallethub.com/edu/best-cities-for-jobs/2173

a company assisting with personal financial improvement, there are smart ways to begin your locational search. If you have location options, their article "2016's Best & Worst Cities to Find a Job," provides analysis of 150 of the most populated U.S. cities across 17 key metrics. The factors considered include such considerations as job opportunities, job growth, salary, affordability, and commute time. Figure 3.1 demonstrates locations of the hottest and coldest job markets in the U.S. during 2016.[1] If ease of finding a position within your selected career field is important to you and you are considering this factor during your departure from the Service, you should look at the complete list to gain a greater understanding.

Highest Number of Job Opportunities (Hottest Job Market)	Lowest Number of Job Opportunities (Coolest Job Market)
1. Salt Lake City, UT	1. Hialeah, FL
1. Cincinnati, OH	2. Fontana, CA
2. Orlando, FL	3. Santa Clarita, CA
3. Irvine, CA	4. Moreno Valley, CA
4. Minneapolis, MN	5. North Las Vegas, NV

Figure 3.1 | Job Market Comparison

Understand Occupational Trends

Similarly, there are huge differences between various occupations regarding growth. Some occupations are booming, while others are on the decline. You want to select a career that has an optimistic outlook for the next 20 years. The BLS provides valuable information online for trends in job growth and wage information for the next 10 years. For the moment, just understand that there will always be jobs available. Individual job growth will be discussed in parallel with each career field, later in this chapter. The question is how well can you compete in the market and are you willing to locate where the jobs are available.

Certifications, Licensure and Education

Most Service members have experience and referential knowledge to transition well into commercial workforce. However, having the right certification, license or degree can make a difference between getting a resume review and not making the cut. Many times, not having the credential screens you away from the competition. It is important to understand the differences.

Education is a pre-requisite for many positions. There are always exceptions. For example, the term engineer is used loosely in some career fields. In fact, some positions state engineer but are really looking for a person with the right experience. But generally, an engineer is going to have a degree in engineering.

Certifications, licenses and accreditations can be a little more difficult to understand.

Certification is the process of publicly attesting or recording that you have achieved or exceeded a specific quality or standard. Professional certification is a voluntary process that identifies and acknowledges that you meet a recognized standard. Certification is nearly always offered by a private, non-governmental agency, which typically are a professional association.

Licensure is a non-voluntary process. A governmental agency regulates a profession and grants permission for you to engage in an occupation. Generally, this license assures that you have obtained the degree of competency required to ensure the public is reasonably protected. It is illegal for anyone to engage in the profession or occupation unless you have a license. State registration and certification are generally somewhat less restrictive than licensing, but there is significant variation from state to state.

Why do you need to know this? Perhaps you have had opportunities to certify or advance your education while in the reserves or on active duty. Maybe you have earned a Project Management Professional (PMP®), Microsoft®, CISCO® or ITIL certification. Having the correct certification is critical to compete for technical jobs in the corporate world. In some career fields, getting certified is one of the best ways to advance your career and assist in finding your transitional job.

Your best bet for career progression is to validate your skills and knowledge by thoughtfully choosing the appropriate certification, license or education that is in demand or required for the career field that is of interest to you. It is one thing to say you have the experience; can you describe your capabilities and what you have done? But you will rarely talk with a hiring manager, if you are screened out by an electronic resume review for not having the required certification, license or education. You will align the appropriate certification, license or education with the career fields that you are moving toward in the career field details section of this chapter.

Certification Methodology

Generally, the certification methodology is very similar across industries. Identify and apply for certification, study or take training, register and pay for the test, take the test and receive your certification. This sounds straightforward, but the process takes time and if you have never certified, it can be a bit intimidating.

Testing Reimbursement
benefits.va.gov/gibill/
licensing_certification.asp

In the past, there have been two major routes for certification. You could pursue certifications out of pocket (individually); or if you were fortunate, get your organization pay for it. Fortunately, as a transitioning Service member, there is a third way to study and gain certification. If you plan accordingly, many certifications are free or at low cost before you leave the Service. It is recommended that you explore the different options and take the available online courses, prior to your departure from the Service. Additionally, funds for training and testing reimbursement are available to you after you leave the Service from the Veterans Administration and G.I. Bill.[2] Regardless, take advantage of every opportunity for education as soon as you can.

COOL

Through the Credentialing Opportunities Online (COOL) program, enlisted soldiers and some warrant officers can learn about various certifications. Both the Army and Marine Corps have COOL websites. The information provides background information on each certification, alignment of the MOS to the certifications, resources to receive reimbursement, and potential training for certification. COOL does not provide credentialing or provide testing. Some of certifications have the exam approved for reimbursement through

COOL, Dude!
Certification
Information:
cool.army.mil
cool.navy.mil
cool.navy.mil/usmc/usn
afvec.langley.af.mil/
afvec/Public/COOL

the G.I. Bill. In some cases, the COOL web site has state-of-the-art, computer-based training available. For example, Figure 3.2 below shows exemplar certification information available through Army COOL for an 11B.

Credential	Certifying Body
Physical Security Professional (PSP)	ASIS International
Certified Sport Security Professional (CSSP)	National Center for Spectator Sports Safety and Security (NCSSSS)
Microsoft Office Specialist (MOS)	Microsoft Corporation
Certified Protection Officer (CPO)	International Foundation for Protection Officers (IFPO)
CompTIA Certified Technical Trainer (CTT+)	Computing Technology Industry Associaion (CompTIA)
IC3 Digital Literacy Certification (IC3)	Certiport
ACSM Certified Personal Trainer (CPT)	American College of Sports Medicine (ACSM)
Automobile/Light Truck - Engine Performance (A8)	National Institute for Automotive Service Excellence (ASE)
Automobile/Light Truck - Engine Repair (A1)	National Institute for Automotive Service Excellence (ASE)
Automobile/Light Truck - Light Vehicle Diesel Engines (A9)	National Institute for Automotive Service Excellence (ASE)
Automobile/Light Truck - Engine Performance (A8)	National Institute for Automotive Service Excellence (ASE)

Figure 3.2 | Exemplar Certification Information - Army COOL - 25B

Career Field Details

This section depicts occupational background information for study and assessment during your transition as each of the five staff functions presented in Chapter 2 (Figure 2.12). These are mapped and detailed in the next sections.

As mentioned earlier, conventional thought believes that Combat Arms Service members could make a great police officer, security guard, SWAT Team member or chief. Should this be your desire, these are highly admirable occupations. Working in the forefront of law enforcement in this day in age is extremely selfless. As you are aware, these occupations can come with high personal risk due to the significant disrespect and discourse by criminal undercurrents of modern society.

However, conventional thought on the transition of Combat Arms professional falls significantly short of understanding the total complexity and capability. You are a leader, a manager, well organized, motivated, task oriented and mission success driven. You will take these skills with you, regardless of the career path you may choose.

The approach taken in this next section, enables the discovery of the many areas you may unknowingly have interest, skills and aptitude. You are the amalgamation of many characteristics and capabilities. You and your experience are unique. Your career path has been like no one else. Reach back during your career and remember the other work related activities, training, experiences and education that you performed over the years. Ask yourself a few questions. Did I enjoy these duties? Is this an area that I am interested in pursuing? Do I believe that I could be happy and successful working in the related career field?

Career Field Alignment

In Chapter 2, you gained an understanding of how your additional duties and staff experience relate to a major staff proponency. It is important that you take a few moments to review Figure 2.10 and understand the alignment of your experiences and additional duties to each staff proponent. This will prove instrumental as we step through the relationship of each staff proponent to the related career fields in the commercial world. Remember, if you truly enjoyed some of these functional skills, you may need to enhance these desires and capabilities with certification or education. You may be able to gain the education or certification prior to leaving the Service. However, depending on your personal financial and educational benefit situation, you may need to support these pursuits by performing a transitional job.

The career field alignment section presents these staff proponents and their functions as they relate to commercial career fields. The five battalion staff functions are presented below in Figure 3.3. There is a significant relationship of each staff proponent to the commercial career fields and occupations. As you read through this next section, you will gain an understanding of the alignment and discern your personal interests.

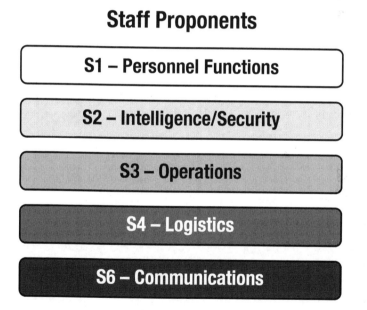

Figure 3.3 | Staff Proponents Career Field Groupings

As we step through the career field alignment to occupations, you will gain insight to how your background may propel you to an exciting commercial career. As shown in Figure 3.4, using the mapping methodology, each staff proponent maps to a potential civilian career fields. These career fields are elaborated with a background description, salary range and occupational outlook. Aligned to each of these career fields are potential occupations for you to consider. Further, a listing of qualification methods is provided. Many of the occupations do not require degrees or certification to obtain entry-level positions based on your experience. However, like your military career, you will only reach your full potential with additional education, certification and/ or training.

Mapping Methodology

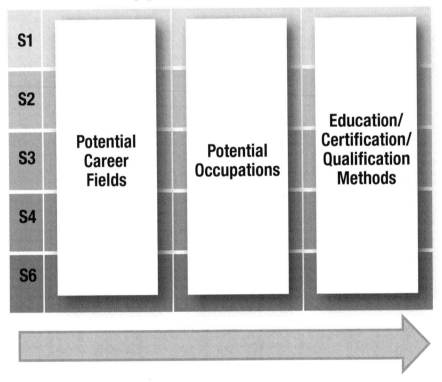

Figure 3.4 | Mapping Methodology

This section acts as a pointer and gives an alignment that arrays your previous work experience to a potential commercial path. Should career fields or occupations spark interest, use these references to assist the initiation of your personal transitional journey. This will enable you to discern career fields and occupations that you would like to learn more about and potentially pursue after the Service. You will then be motivated to perform the research and the effort required to get you to your goal. Research the job titles you find of interest and look for various jobs around the country to learn about the associated descriptions, specific requirements, duties and pay of the individual position. This represents the beginning of your in-depth research required to obtain a position that you find desirable.

Based upon your considerable experience in the Service, you will soon realize there are many more post-military career options than what you currently believe. We know conventional wisdom would place us in a box. However, there is much more to you than many believe. Now you need to believe that as well! Study and begin to chart your course using the personal strategic road map provided in this book. Let's begin with the S1 and personnel career field.

S1 – Personnel Career Field (See pg. 33)
Background

If you have experience performing tasks or additional duties in the S1 arena, you should consider yourself fortunate. Potentially more than any other function, the S1 maps neatly to civilian occupations. If you enjoyed your work as an S1, a retention NCO, a recruiter or duties in the orderly room or battalion staff preparing awards, UCMJ actions, pay inquiries or evaluations you may be a perfect candidate for HR in the commercial world.

People who have human resources careers are the liaison of the business world. They must balance the representation of the worker and management. Sometimes they work for a specific company to match people with positions, but many provide HR services to other companies. Personnel managers recruit and screen applicants and are sometimes involved in the interview process, too.

In the commercial world, they take care of payroll and benefits paperwork and connect employees to management.

In general, employers like candidates with a bachelor's degree when hiring for HR positions. Coursework in business, accounting and professional writing will be enablers. However, experience can be a plus when interviewing for human resources careers. Written appropriately on your resume, your experience in the orderly room, personnel section or S1, may result in an entry-level HR position. Consider obtaining a human resource certification; as this will assist your understanding of your skills, provide new commercial skills, so that you can delineate your capabilities for the hiring officials. Even if you land an entry level HR position through certification, you should still plan on pursuing your degree as it may take years on the job to gain the experience to move up the ladder.

Outlook & Salaries

There are significant job outlook variations within the personnel career field, depending on the specialty you desire to pursue. The BLS reports that the basic HR job duties are essentially the same, but the number of jobs and the projected growth for HR specialists and HR managers are different. In 2012 there were a reported 495,500 Specialists jobs with a projected growth of eight percent by 2022. Comparatively, the 2012 number for managers was only 102,700, but the expected increase is larger: 13 percent over the next 10 years.

There are also significant differences in salary within the HR roles. Managers earn almost twice as much as HR specialists. This is because HR managers have the added responsibility of consulting with businesses' top executives regarding the company's labor needs and budget. For these extra duties, managers' median salaries in 2012 were approximately $99,720 annually compared to specialists' average wages at $55,640.

BLS Website:
bls.gov/home.htm

Other roles, such as the contract, legal and financial management vary greatly regarding outlook and salaries. For example, with a slightly higher median salary ($103,460)[3], the legal industry has over 1,125,000 people employed nationwide, but is not expected to have a lot of growth.[4] For more detailed and up to date information on each role and job listed below, check out the U.S. Department of Labor, BLS website.

Figure 3.5, describes the S1 functions as they relay to the commercial personnel field. You will find the major roles with their descriptions along with specific jobs. As always you are encouraged to pursue additional information on those areas that you find of interest. Reference are given for additional research, which can be found in the end notes.

PERSONNEL CAREER FIELD

If you are thinking about working in the personnel career field, there are many career paths to choose from. You can stay a generalist and climb the career ladder into a management role, or you can distill the aspects of the career you like best—teaching people, negotiating, the technical aspects, etc.—and become a niche specialist. Bottom line: if you enjoyed working with soldiers and marines to help them resolve their personal problems, this may be the career field for you.

ROLE: HUMAN RESOURCE MANAGEMENT

HR management is the management of human resources or the people who make up the workforce of an organization. HR is the function in organizations designed to maximize employee performance in support of the organizational strategic objectives. HR major concern is the management of people within organizations, focusing on policies and on associated systems. HR departments assume responsibility for several activities, including employee benefits design, employee recruitment, "training and development," performance appraisal, and rewarding (e.g., managing pay and benefit systems). HR also has over watch for organizational change and industrial relations. One of the challenges is balancing organizational practices with requirements arising from collective bargaining (unions), regulatory and legal standards.

EDUCATION AND CERTIFICATION

Generally, a bachelor's degree is required for this role in HR, Management, Education, Training and Development, or Industrial and Labor Relations. With experience/certification you can enter as a human resources specialist. Certifications include Professional in Human Resources (PHR) & Senior Professional in Human Resources (SPHR), International Foundation of Employee Benefit Plans (IFEBP) Certification. Certifications such as insurance industry certification in workers' compensation and regulatory certifications in such for various state workers' compensation certification may be appropriate for your field.

OCCUPATIONS

Human Resource Specialist	Benefits Specialist
Human Resource Manager	Workman's Compensation Administrator
Staffing and Recruiting Specialist	Training and Development Manager
Employee and Labor Relations	Payroll Specialist / Manager
Workforce Analyst	

FIG 3.5

ROLE: LEGAL INDUSTRY

Have you been involved in putting together or executing UCMJ actions? The legal industry is thriving and a there has never been a better time to embark on a legal career. Often a concern, many legal careers do not require a law degree. Legal services are complex and require a team of capable professionals to provide quality and cost-effective service. Thus, the legal field holds hundreds of legal career options encompassing a diverse range of skills, experience and education. Developments in technology and its application are also creating new legal career opportunities.

EDUCATION AND CERTIFICATION

Many of these jobs do not require a bachelor's degree, but many many have other requirements, consistent with achieving paralegal or legal service certification. Additionally, universities like Kaiser and Drexel offer certificates at the graduate and undergraduate level in such areas as Criminal Law, Entrepreneurship Law and Compliance areas such as Health Care, Human Resource and Higher Education. Ultimately, a bachelor's degree in pre-law, criminal justice or related field may be the path towards upward mobility.

The National Association of Legal Assistants (NALA) among other organizations, offers paralegal certification. For those desiring to become lawyers, the Juris Doctor degree or Doctor of Law degree (J.D.), is the professional doctorate required to practice law in the US. A bachelor's degree is required for admission into a JD program. The LSAT is an integral part of the law school admission process in the United States. The JD program is generally a three-year, full-time academic program. All US states accept graduation from an American Bar Association approved law school as meeting that state's education requirement for eligibility to sit for the bar examination.

OCCUPATIONS

Legal Billing Specialis
Legal Secretary
Law Library Assistant
Administrative Law Judge
Arbitrator
Attorney
Corrections Officer
Court Recorder or Messenger
Law Library Assistant

Compliance Specialist
Conflicts Analyst
File Clerk
Courtroom Deputy /Bailiff
Legislative Staffer
Legal Analyst
Lobbyist
Court Administration Specialist

ROLE: SALES/ MARKETING

As a recruiter, you may have discovered a magical mix of skills and personality that a career in selling requires. As you are aware, you may be able to earn yourself a six-figure salary in sales; but not all sales positions are that glamorous and high-paying. According to BLS in 2014, the occupations with the largest employment were retail salespersons and cashiers, per the BLS. These two occupations combined make up nearly 6% of total employment in the United States. Unfortunately, they are among the lowest paid sales occupations. Sales engineers top the list for pay, unseating securities, commodities, and financial services sales agents with mean annual salaries of $104,660. These sales professionals generally sell for complex scientific and technological products or services to businesses.

EDUCATION AND CERTIFICATION

You can find positions within retail sales that require no education. Others require extensive knowledge and certification. Sales representative of wholesale, manufacturing, technical and scientific products must have extensive knowledge of the products' parts and functions and must understand the scientific processes that make these products work. Selling securities or commodities in investment and trading firms, could take several years of study and certification. The good news is that some investment houses will assist in this training for the right candidate. If education is a challenge, as an alternative to retail sales, real estate brokers or real estate agents have a very popular and rewarding business. Even though there is some variation by state, a real estate agent must be 18 years of age, with high school diploma and obtain a real estate license. Google and Facebook among others offer certifications for digital marketing.

OCCUPATIONS

Sales Representative
Sales Engineer
Advertising Sales Agent
Supervisor of Non-Retail Sales Workers
Real Estate Agent / Broker Cashier

Securities / Commodities Sales
Retail Sales
Cashier
Securities / Commodities Sales

ROLE: CONTRACT MANAGEMENT

You may have received training or experience as a contracting representative in uniform. Both the government and the commercial world require contract management. Contract management skills are developed through time, with continuing education and practice. A successful contract manager has developed skills in three main areas: technical, conceptual, and human relations. Technical skills include preparing and issuing solicitations, preparing bids and proposals, preparing / analyzing terms and conditions and analyzing procurement requirements and supplier capabilities. The conceptual skills are critical as you must be able to visualize the contract's capability, organization, operations, while pursuing the strategic goals and objectives of the agency or company. The human relations aspect is critical, as your performance will require collaborative interaction and cooperation of many people whom you have no organizational control. Working with government and contractor representatives requires solid interpersonal and communication skills.[6] All jobs within this category require different variations and experience of these skills.

EDUCATION AND CERTIFICATION

You do not have to acquire a degree for entry-level positions within this career field. Experience will be of great assistance, but for career development you need training. Training for these skills can be accomplished in degree, certificate, professional continuing education, or specialized programs. The National Contract Management Association (NCMA) offers certification in multiple areas such as the Contract Body of Knowledge and the Federal Acquisition Regulation. However, it is far less expensive to get Defense Acquisition Workforce Improvement Act (DAWIA) certified prior to your departure from the Service. If you become employed as a DoD civil servant, you will be able to obtain DAWIA certification at no cost. Another great certification that will get you in the door is the PMP or Program Management Professional (PgMP) from PMI.

OCCUPATION

Contracting Officer
Contracts Administrator
Contracts Specialist
Pricing Specialist
Proposal Manager

Business Developer
Capture Manager
Project Manager
Task Lead

ROLE: FINANCE

You have performed budgeting for office supplies and expenditures; while navigating the maze of rules that allow people to use the Government Purchase Card. You have helped with pay inquiries. A career in finance is not necessarily all about money. You need to have a good understanding of people and the associated psychology. Most will obtain a business degree, but it is not required to be successful in some of the associated jobs. The finance sector offers a variety of positions catering to several different skills and interests.

Corporate finance jobs involve working for a company in the capacity of finding and managing the capital necessary to run the enterprise. Commercial banking, is a critical field, offering a range of financial services, from savings and checking accounts to IRAs and loans. Investment-banking jobs deal with facilitating the issuance of corporate securities and making these securities available for investors to purchase, all while trading securities and providing financial advice to both corporations and wealthy individual investors.[7] Among all the jobs in the financial industry, the fastest growing is financial advisory jobs. Driving this growth are the baby boomers, seeking advice as they navigate retirement. The decline in pension funds also compels younger workers to contact personal financial advisors.[8]

EDUCATION AND CERTIFICATION

Depending on the job, position and corporation, you do not have to acquire a degree for entry level positions within this career field. Gaining licenses and/or certifications to understand and sell financial products, mixed with a great attitude and concern for clients, has led many professionals becoming wealthy selling insurance or commodities. However, to gain a true understanding of the financial sector and to enable your personal professional growth in the financial industry, you will need to obtain a business degree.

OCCUPATIONS

Hedge Fund Analyst
Investment Banker
Corporate Finance
Regulatory compliance officer
Personal Financial Advisors
Financial Analysts
Insurance Sales Agents
Securities, Commodities and
    Financial Services Sales Agents

Budget Analysts
Financial Managers
Insurance Sales / Underwriting
Insurance Sales
Actuary / Financial Risk Manager
Auditor
Accounting

S2 - Intelligence and Security Career Field
Background

Have you had the opportunity to work with intelligence at battalion or brigade level? Maybe you had associates or friends that did and you often were curious about how they did their work analyzing situations in foreign countries. Maybe you have been asked to decipher elements from a drone feed based on what you saw on the ground. You might have interpreted interrogations or radio transmissions, or played a role in aggregating information from various sources.

If you have enjoyed working in and around the intelligence field and the associated experiences you have gained, you will find a multitude of choices when it comes to translating your military experience into a degree or career selection.[9] Your travels have provided unique educational experiences. Coupling your understanding of political systems, geography, history and trends across the world with a degree in political science, business or finance will enable your career in the rapidly growing global business community.

Your skills in communication, negotiation, mediation, and facilitation need to be leveraged when searching for your new career. Your ability to aggregate and translate intelligence into meaningful reports is an extraordinary asset your resume must highlight. These skills translate into commercial career fields involving business analysis and intelligence, investigations and detective services, records management, advertisement and design. Within the government, you could perform these similar duties across most agency or you could migrate toward any of the three letter agencies (FBI, CIA, DHS, etc.) as an analyst, operator or agent. DoD contract organizations are constantly looking for these highly-specialized skills.

Within the federal government, there are 17 agencies such as DIA, CIA, FBI, etc., that make up the Intelligence Community (IC). The overall efforts of the IC are administered by the Office of the Director of National Intelligence (ODNI). ODNI's role is to organize and

Federal Intelligence Careers:
Intelligencecareers.gov/index.html

coordinate the efforts of the IC agencies. Those agencies are divided into three groups:

- Program managers, who advise and assist the ODNI in identifying requirements, developing budgets, managing finances and evaluating the IC's performance

- Departmentals, which are IC components within government departments outside of the DoD that focus on serving their parent department's intelligence needs

- Services, which encompass intelligence personnel in the armed forces, and which primarily support their own Service branch's needs[10]

If gathering, analyzing, or evaluating information from various sources, such as law enforcement databases, intelligence networks, surveillance, or geographic information systems to anticipate and prevent organized crime activities or terrorism sounds like an interesting second career, then read on.

Outlook & Salaries

Jobs and salaries in the intelligence field continue to grow. For example, nationwide vacancies for intelligence analysts have increased by 27 percent over the last 10 years, with an average growth of 4.55 percent per year. Demand for intelligence analysts is expected continue, with an expected 20,300 new jobs filled by 2018, representing an annual increase of 2.29 percent over the next few years.[11]

Other roles, such as the detective, investigator, business analyst or marketing vary greatly regarding outlook and salaries. For example, the market research analysts have an average salary of over $62,000 per year. But this job has an expected growth rate of over 19%, which is much faster than average.[12] For more detailed and up to date information on each role and job listed below, visit the US Department of Labor, BLS website.

BLS Website:
bls.gov/home.htm

Figure 3.6, describes the S2 functions as they relate to the intelligence and security career field. You will find the major roles with their descriptions. Further, specific jobs within each major role are given. As always you are encouraged to pursue additional information on those areas that are of interest to you. References are provided for additional research.

INTELLIGENCE AND SECURITY CAREER FIELD

The intelligence and security career field focuses on an ever-expanding range of issues, from terrorist financing, drug trafficking, environmental issues, foreign technology threats and nuclear proliferation. The government and the business world need analyst to assist in the determination of a plethora of problems, developing solutions to counteract the associated challenges, and executing counter measures to resolve the issues.

ROLE: BUSINESS ANALYST

You have participated in threat assessments. Those threat assessments are the rudimentary elements required to build a career in Homeland Security. The federal government and many commercial firms are looking for specialists in threat assessments and foreign analysis to help them make future business plans. These skills are hard to attain in the commercial world. Your experience working with aggregation tools, developing dashboards, scorecards, reports, and creating analytics are essential elements for your resume.

Businesses need to understand the threats and how to exploit the available business information. In our global economy, they need know which governments are friendly, which countries are safe, and how best to interact global customers and threats to ensure a safe and profitable working environment.

EDUCATION AND CERTIFICATION

You won't necessarily need a degree, but getting one in finance, information systems, business, or accounting, will hasten your advancement. You will need to know how to aggregate information. Therefore, certification like Certified Business Analysis Professional™ (CBAP®) from International Institute of Business Analysis (IIBA) or Professional Business Analyst (PBA) from PMI will be invaluable.

OCCUPATIONS

Business Threat Analyst	Risk Manager
Physical Security Analyst	Business Threat Analyst
Business Analyst	Sales Analyst
Business Intelligence Analyst	Market Research Analysts
Business Management Analyst	

ROLE: DETECTIVE / INVESTIGATOR

Do you like solving puzzles? Have you had to solve some during your military career? Logic skills and an understanding of alternative solutions are required to be a successful investigator. Solving puzzles is an important part of the job, regardless of your desired occupation within this career field. Understanding the forensic processes and results gives investigators a leg up on closing cases. Investigators are numerous today. Fraud, crime and quality issues abound and must be mediated, arbitrated and resolved. To ensure that happens correctly with thorough due diligence, an investigator or detective is required. Detectives and investigators fall into two categories; public or private. Public detectives are often law enforcement agents, investigating criminal related activities. Private detectives or investigators may work for individuals and such issues as investigating stolen property or missing persons. They may be employed by large corporations, working on fraud or theft, by example.[13]

EDUCATION AND CERTIFICATION:

A degree is not universally required. However, most law enforcement agencies typically desire candidates with degrees. Criminal justice programs are offered through most colleges, universities; with brick and mortar and online options.

You are required to have a license. Licensing is a matter of passing a certification exam. There is study required to taking the exam, but many courses of study prepare students in a few months. DTI (Detective Training Institute) in California offers a preparation course for the licensing exam.[14] If you desire to become some other type of inspector, you will need a license as well. Inspection Certification Associates (ICA) is a provider of online Home Inspection Training and Certification.[15]

OCCUPATIONS

Police Detective
Private Investigator
Forensic Science Technicians
Homicide Investigator
Fire Inspector
Claims Adjuster, Appraiser, Examiners
Insurance Fraud Investigator
Arbitrators / Mediator

Information Security (see S6)
Quality Control Inspector
IRS Agent / Examiner
Environmental Protection Officer
Occupational Health and Safety Specialist
Accountants and Auditors (see S1)
Construction / Building Inspector
Home / Real Estate Inspector

ROLE: GOVERNMENT ANALYST/AGENCIES

Your military Service could qualify you to continue to serve our nation at the Federal Bureau of Investigation (FBI), the Central Intelligence Agency (CIA), the Department of Homeland Security (DHS) and even the Internal Revenue Service (IRS). Opportunities for qualified applicants are available in the U.S. and many locations overseas. These agencies recognize your values and service and offers many opportunities for your continued career growth. If you join one of the agencies you will have opportunities to work in one of many disciplines, ranging from special agent, analyst or technician; while working in professional capacities that will meet your personal interests and experiences. All the government agencies strongly urge military and veterans to apply to the positions that interest them. The other great news is that your time in Service counts towards benefits and retirement within the federal government. If you are currently pursuing a degree program, the agencies have student opportunities with paid student internship, scholarship and co-op programs. Visit the following web sites to learn more about how your time in the Service enables your job search within these agencies:

DHS: dhs.gov/homeland-security-careers/veterans
FBI: fbijobs.gov/veterans
CIA: cia.gov/careers/military-transition
IRS: jobs.irs.gov/resources/equal-opportunity/veteran-hiring

EDUCATION AND CERTIFICATION:

With government employment in this field, your experience counts. You can get entry-level government jobs based on your experience without a degree. However, you will need to obtain a degree if you desire to climb the civil service ladder. Typically, you will seek a degree in the career areas that you desire to pursue. Criminal Law, Political science and economics or finance are all great degrees that will move you forward within these organizations. The websites listed above will assist you in this determination.

OCCUPATIONS

Statistical Analyst
Special Agent
Investigator / Investigative Analyst
Document Analyst
Intelligence Aid and Clerk Series
Communications Clerk / Analyst
Intelligence Analyst

Cartographer
Navigational Information Analyst
Inspection, Investigation, Enforcement, and
    Compliance Officer
Correctional Officer
Criminal Investigator

ROLE: MANAGEMENT ANALYST

These respected analysts propose ways to improve an organization's effectiveness and efficiency. They advise managers on how to make organizations more profitable through reduced costs and increased revenues. These analyst interview personnel, conducting onsite observations to determine the methods, equipment, and personnel that need improvement. They analyze data such as revenue, expenditure, and employment reports.

They organize this information about organizational problem(s) or "pain points" that need to be corrected, often providing the procedure or road to improvement. Using techniques such as "value stream analysis" they develop and recommend new solutions, alternative practices, recommend new systems, procedures, or organizational changes to management through presentations or written reports. They follow up with management to ensure the desired effects are occurring, after the change. Some management analysts work directly for organizations they analyze. However, many work as consultants on a contractual basis. Some projects require a team of consultants, each specializing in one area. Other management consultants work independently with client managers.

EDUCATION AND CERTIFICATION

This field usually requires a bachelor's degree in business, management, process improvement or similar field and several years of experience is required. A Master's degree is often preferred. The Certified Management Consultant (CMC) designation and Six Sigma or Lean Six Sigma green or black belt certification will improve job prospects.

OCCUPATIONS

Management Consulting
Product Analyst
Program Analyst
Market Research Analysts
Operations Research Analysts
Financial Analyst / Managers (See S1)

Budget Analysts (See S1)
Accountants and Auditors (See S1)
Workforce Analyst (See S1)
Supply Chain Analyst (See S4)
Forecast and Demand Planning Analyst

ROLE: ADVERTISING, DESIGN AND MARKETING

At first glance, advertising may seem like a strange translation for someone with a military intelligence background. However, it is a very good fit. To successfully work in the intelligence field, you need to know and understand the people and their mental thought processes that you are collecting information and performing analysis. You must understand their cultural values, their wants and their needs. This is the way advertising agencies and companies perform work daily. This is the kind of information they need to know about their target audiences. You already know how to collect these facts out and analyze them for mission success.[16] Therefore, you may be a good fit for this line of work.

EDUCATION AND CERTIFICATION

Many of these occupations require degrees or certification, but not all. For example, advertising managers often possess a 4-year bachelor's degree in advertising or a related field such as journalism or marketing. However, per O*Net Online in 2010, 54% of advertising managers held a bachelor's degree, and 22% of workers held an associate's degree and 14% had some college, but no degree.[17] There are a multitude of certifications such as Certified E-Marketing Analyst from the Institute of Certified E-Commerce Consultants, if you choose to enhance or show your capabilities.

OCCUPATIONS

Advertising Managers
Promotions Manager
Marketing Manager
Graphics Designer
Art Director

Market Research Analyst
Brand Manager
Media Buyer
Meeting, Convention and Event Planners

S3 – Operations and Training
Background

Just as your military training developed your skills, most of us had significant leadership and management opportunity. You are a good leader. In the commercial world, the best managers are also great leaders. However, finding great managers who are great leaders is not so common. Therefore, if you can do both well, you will be successful as a civilian.

Management or administration of an organization, could be for a business, non-profit or government body. Much of management's effort is devoted to setting strategy, goals and objectives for the organization and coordinating the efforts of employees and many times volunteers. Successful managers accomplish the organization's objectives through the careful application of available resources, such as financial, natural, technological, and HR.

In the military, the term operations is used to define many things.

Operations and management are closely related. As you make your transition to the commercial world, it is important to understand the difference between operations and project management. Operations are continuous, repetitive and ongoing activities in many organizations and include such functions as manufacturing, accounting, finance, or production. Projects are specific tasks that have a beginning and an end. This includes implementations, developing a new product, or construction.

For the commercial work force, important degrees in management are the Bachelor of Business and Master of Business Administration (MBA). For the public sector, the Master of Public Administration (MPA) is a similar degree tailored for management within state, local or federal government sectors.

In large organizations, you will typically find three levels of management. Senior management, such as the board of directors, corporate officers or president of an organization, set the strategic goals of the organization and determine how the organization will operate. Senior managers provide direction to middle managers. In turn, middle managers, (branch managers, regional managers and section managers), provide direction to front-line managers. Middle managers communicate the strategic goals of senior management to the front-line managers. Supervisors and front-line team leaders, report to middle management. They oversee the work of employees or volunteers and provide direction on day to day tasks.

In smaller organizations, you will find the scope of manager to be much wider. You may find yourself performing several roles found in a large organization. As you are probably aware, small organizations outnumber larger ones, tenfold.

Outlook

Organizations are flatter than they were 30 years ago. This means span of control for managers is growing. U.S. corporate hierarchies have become flatter over the past twenty years, per research from the National Bureau of Economic Research. This is not exactly earth shattering, but this would have an effect on outlook. Chief Executive Officers (CEOs) are increasing the number of managers who report directly to the top while there has been a reduction in the ranks of middle managers. Therefore, just a few years ago, management was an evaporating occupation.[18]

However, it has become apparent that productivity requires high quality operational managers, and outlook is not pessimistic. Employment of management occupations is projected to grow 6 percent from 2014 to 2024, which is about average for all occupations. This 6 percent growth will result in about 500,000 new jobs over the next 8-10 years. Per the BLS, this growth will be driven by the formation of new organizations and expansion of existing ones, which will require more personnel to manage these operations.[19]

Salaries

The median annual wage for operations and management occupations was $98,560 in May 2015, which was the highest wage of all the major occupational groups.[20] Due to organizational flattening, salary and bonuses across the hierarchy are growing as well as incentive pay.

BLS Website:
bls.gov/home.htm

Specific roles, such as the food service or lodging managers require no formal degree, and pay around $50,000, with average growth (5-7 percent). Training and development managers will make $102,640, slightly higher than the national average with 8 percent growth. For more detailed and up to date information on each role and job listed below, check out the U.S. Department of Labor, BLS website.

To gain a better understanding of the S3 functions as they relay to the operations and training career field, review Figure 3.7 below. You will find the major roles with their descriptions. Further, specific jobs within each major role are given. As always you are encouraged to pursue additional information on those operational areas that are of interest to you. References are given for additional research.

OPERATIONS AND TRAINING

You know your operational experience is perfect for management. You have been managing personnel for many years. Developing plans and schedules, executing plans and making checklists are second nature to you. Chances are you already know how to seek and visualize the big picture. Developing strategy and budgets, all while managing employees and their schedules comes naturally as well. You have developed and conducted individual and classroom training. It is time to take your operations and training capabilities to the commercial world. Once you learn the industry vernacular, you will find that your adaptability and can-do attitude highly desirable amongst employers.

ROLE: OPERATIONS MANAGER

Operations managers are the go-to personnel in a business. The operations manager helps various departments within a company coordinate to meet the mission or strategic goals of the company. Regardless of size, every business and organization needs them, regardless of industry or sector. These critical managers plan, direct and coordinate the operations of public or private sector organizations. Duties and responsibilities include formulating policies, managing daily operations, and planning the use of materials and HR, but are too diverse and general in nature to classify in any one functional area of management or administration, such as personnel, purchasing, or administrative services. Excludes First-Line Supervisors.[21] The operations manager is found in many industries to include: corporate industry, restaurants, government, scientific and technical, consulting and computer design.

EDUCATION AND CERTIFICATION

Occupations such as hotel management and restaurant management will not require a degree. But the others on this list will require a degree in business or operations management.

OCCUPATIONS

Director of Operations	Manager / Assistant Manager
Facility Manager	Plant Manager
Territory / Regional Manager	Operations Supervisor
Chief Operations Officer	Production Manager
Operations Support Manager	Hotel Manager
Retail Manager	VP Operations
Associate Director of Operations	

ROLE: FOOD SERVICE AND LODGING MANAGERS

Food service managers are responsible for the daily operation of restaurants and other establishments that prepare and serve food and beverages. They direct staff to ensure that customers are satisfied with their dining experience. Similarly, lodging managers ensure that guests on vacation or business travel have a pleasant experience at a hotel, motel, resort or other types of establishment with accommodations. They also ensure that the establishment is run efficiently and profitably. Both functions balance customer relations and the business to ensure profitability.[22]

EDUCATION AND CERTIFICATION:

Entry-level management positions do not required college. However, today more professionals within the industry are gaining degrees in hospitality, hotel management and culinary certifications.

OCCUPATIONS

Guest Services Manager.
Food and Beverage Manager.
Executive Meeting Manager.
Housekeeping Supervisor.
Catering Manager.
Cafe Manager

Catering Sales Manager.
Room Service Manager.
Resort/Time Share Sales Director
Cruise Ship Lodging Director
Vacation Package Sales Director
Meeting, Convention, and Event Planners

ROLE: BUSINESS MANAGEMENT

You have gained significant information about foreign countries, nation building and development. You have in-depth knowledge about political situations, governmental friendliness to foreign investment and grounding in various local customs. Not only do you have the background information for global business management, you also understand the situation overseas and at home. You can bring those various areas of knowledge together with a degree in business management or global business management, enabling your value through level your experience and knowledge.[23]

EDUCATION AND CERTIFICATION:

Bachelors or Masters in Business, Finance, Accounting, Management. There are various certifications such as Certified Public Accountant (CPA), Program Management (PgMP) from PMI. For Insurance underwriting, consider the Insurance Institute of America, as they offer designations such as an Associate in Commercial Underwriting (ACU) and an Associate in Personal Insurance (API).

OCCUPATIONS

Medical and Health Services Manager
Appraisers and Assessors of Real Estate
Budget Analysts
Buyers and Purchasing Agents
Claims Adjusters, Appraisers,
   Examiners, and Investigators
Cost Estimators

Financial Analysts
Financial Examiners
Insurance Underwriters
Management Analysts
Program Manager, Business
   Unit Director, C-Level Officer
Industrial Production Manager

ROLE: PROJECT MANAGEMENT

If you enjoyed planning, scheduling and executing operations, your future career path could very well be project management. Experts in the field believe that military are well suited for the career field of project management. Your leadership and planning skills ingrained during military Service, and your adaptability to change, will enable you to successfully transition into a great career field like project management. Action officer, training officer, operations planner, commander, platoon sergeant, are all military terms that equate to project manager in the commercial world. Therefore, the project management career field is a high-value, target rich environment for you to consider. PMI states that project managers are change agents, making project goals their own, while using their skills and expertise to inspire a sense of shared purpose within the project team. Project managers enjoy new challenges and thrive on driving business results.[24] Project management spans all industries. Typically, a project manager would have skills in construction, IT, health care, finance or a multitude of other industries.

EDUCATION AND CERTIFICATION

You do not need a degree to be a project manager, but you do need experience. If you have a degree, it is easier to demonstrate your experience during the certification process. The PMP, which is the anchor certification for PMI, recognizes demonstrated experience, skill and performance in leading and directing projects. Anyone who desires recognition in the competence of performing in the role of a PM, specifically experience in leading and directing projects, and meets the requisites should apply for this coveted credential. As you mature in your project management skills, or if you have already had programmatic experience, you may wish to pursue a Program Management Certification (PgMP). The PgMP exam tests the ability, knowledge and experience of program management.[25] An excellent resource for learning more about this exciting career field is the book titled "The Transitioning Military Project Manager."

OCCUPATIONS

Project Coordinator
Project Expeditor
Project Manager
Program Manager
Portfolio Manager
Scheduler / Master Scheduler

Quality Manager
Risk Manager
PMO Manager
Agile Manager
Product Manager

ROLE: TRAINING AND DEVELOPMENT

Ongoing professional development and training is a requirement in all organizations to include the corporate world, nonprofits, educational institutions, and public service agencies. Training takes many forms, from individualized coaching to group mentoring to online instruction. In this role, you will plan, direct, or coordinate the training and development activities and staff of an organization. You may find yourself developing and coordinating implementation of curriculum, planning, organizing, and conducting teacher training conferences or workshops, analyzing student test data, assessing and discussing implementation of curriculum standards with school staff, reviewing and recommending textbooks and other educational materials, recommending teaching techniques and the use of different or new technologies, developing procedures for teachers to implement curriculum, training teachers and other instructional staff in new content or programs, mentoring or coaching teachers to improve their skills.

EDUCATION AND CERTIFICATION

If you pursue this role, you will probably need to get an advanced degree such as Masters in Curriculum Development & Instructional Technology, Master's in Training and Development, Industrial Education, or a certificate of curriculum developer. With the rapid growth of online training, you may desire to pursue course authoring software training and certification, such as industry leaders Articulate Storyline and iSpring Suite.

OCCUPATIONS

Teachers
Instructional Coordinator
Curriculum developer
Training and Development Manager
Industrial Trainer / Developer
Junior ROTC Instructor (Army, Navy, Air Force)
Veteran Transition Specialist
Consultant

ROLE: PUBLIC RELATIONS

Do you have the gift of gab or a silver tongue? Do you know how to think quickly? Can you speak plainly? Are you able to capture the right sound bite while relaying the facts? Public Relations (PR) is all about planning, directing and coordinating activities to create or maintain a favorable public image or raise awareness of issues associated with their organizations or clients. If you are engaged in fundraising, you will find yourself planning and coordinating activities to solicit "gifts" or funds for special projects or nonprofit organizations such as colleges and universities. Companies now put tremendous value in keeping their on-line image untarnished, requiring a significant number of social media experts in the PR field. Regardless of role, this is a very public position and requires great personality and charisma for success.

EDUCATION AND CERTIFICATION:

A degree in public relations, communications, broadcast journalism, or similar area is necessary. You need to be well versed in such areas as persuasion strategies, communication and public relations theory, relationship building, societal trends, ethical and legal issues. There are certifications for Certified Public Relations Specialist (CPRS). The Public Relations Society of America (PRSA) offers more background for those desiring to enter this field.[26]

OCCUPATIONS

Public Relations Specialist
Public Relations Manager
Fund Raising Manager
Director of Gifts
Press Secretary
Agency Spokesperson
PR / Marketing Coordinator
Community Association Manager
Consumer Advocate

Customer Relations
Communications Officer
Director of Communications
Social Media Specialist
Conversion Optimization Specialist
Public Safety Emergency Communications
  Specialist
Community Relations Manager
Journalism

ROLE: PUBLIC SERVICES

Professional public service today offers many career opportunities including those in governments at all levels, in nonprofit organizations and Non-Governmental Organizations (NGOs), in higher education, and in private sector companies that work under contract to governments. These opportunities provide good pay and benefits, numerous choices of where to work in the United States and around the world, and resources for further training and education. In the past, a public service career meant government employment, today there is a significant connection between governments, nonprofits, NGOs, the private sector, and universities. Employment within any of these organizations can produce highly productive careers which contribute directly to the public good. Your service to the nation is a known commodity and many organizations and programs such as the Troops to Teachers program assist in easing your transition into the public education system, so that you can continue to provide service to our educational system, rapidly.

EDUCATION AND CERTIFICATION:

Various levels of education are required. You certainly can enter many of these fields with a high school diploma. However, you will want to obtain a bachelors or advanced degree if you desire to continue your professional growth and development.

OCCUPATIONS

Emergency Management Specialist / Director
EMT / Paramedic
Corrections Officer
Police Officer / Fireman

Rehabilitation Officer / Counselor
Records Management
Postal Worker / Manager
Educator
Pastor / Ministry

S4 – Logistics
Background

As you prepare to depart the Service, your future career path could very well be a logistics professional in the commercial or public sector. You may have received expert training from the military that is well suited for the career field of commercial logistics. Your Combat Arms experience likely required you to learn logistics skills and responsibility. You may have supervised and performed logistics functions many times during your career. You probably ordered supplies, stocked and issued repair parts, clothing and general supplies utilizing the supply system. You have possibly been responsible for transaction follow up and receipt procedures, how to enhance warehouse layout and storage, and the proper operation of the Government Purchase Card Program. You likely have driven countless miles, performed duties associated with hazardous material control and management or maintained inventory databases for material stocked in warehouses and shipboard storerooms. You may have had On-the-Job Training (OJT) on how to maintain financial records and accounting systems. These are examples of the variety and expansive world of logistics, even if you were in a non-logistical career field. If you find these functions interesting and desire to pursue logistics as a potential post-military career, then keep reading and learn how your skills may apply.

Logistics is a growing industry with career field potential in the commercial world. Companies continue to send manufacturing overseas while outsourcing production, consistently providing rewards for logistics providers. Logistics is key to moving this overseas production into and around our country. Globalization continues to push companies to streamline their logistics process to remain competitive. One of the windfalls within the logistics industry is the continued training of logistics workers. Continuing education, certifications and OJT are great enablers.

Military veterans with some experience and/or education in supply and transportation can transition into the commercial logistics management field and it is certainly a possible commercial career field move. Therefore, a significant number of NCOs are great candidates for this profession. Logistics management tends to be cross functional with a wider view of the operations and total logistics function of the organization.

There are three major logistics career fields. These are supply, transportation and supply chain or logistics management. You may be asking "Where is maintenance?" Maintenance is absorbed with in the previously mentioned logistics career field and in many other commercial settings. To dig deeper and receive more in-depth information and analysis of this career field along with your many options, make sure you read *"The Transitioning Military Logistician."*

Outlook & Salaries

As this industry continues to enjoy unfettered global growth, the median pay for logistician managers with a bachelor's degree is around $72,780 per year. Further, the outlook through 2025 indicates 21% growth, far better than the national outlook average of 11%.[27] Warehouse workers and truck drivers should meet the national average growth rate. Understandably, not all occupations within the logistics career field will enjoy this positive outlook. For example, purchasing managers and material clerks are not predicted to keep up with the average growth rate.

Relating the S4 functions to commercial logistics can be done from by reviewing Figure 3.8, below. You will find the major roles with their descriptions. Further, specific jobs within each major role are given. An additional way to gain a more in-depth understanding of the commercial logistics career field, is by reading

BLS Website:
bls.gov/home.htm

"The Transitioning Military Logistician" which is part of the *"Transitioning Military Series."* If you decide to take a deeper dive into commercial logistics understanding, much of the research has already been performed for you. For more detailed and up to date information on each role and job listed below, check out the U.S. Department of Labor, BLS website.

LOGISTICS

There are three major logistics career fields. These are supply, transportation and supply chain or logistics management. In the commercial world, maintenance is absorbed with in the previously mentioned logistics career field and in many other commercial settings. However, it is broken into a separate and distinct section below.

ROLE: SUPPLY Within the supply chain and warehouses, there are many worker and management positions. Employees will be engaged working or managing these systems and have a specific function within the supply chain. Generally, military veterans transition into commercial supply easily due to their skills and training in the Service. Therefore, if you like working as a warehouse associate or order processor, you are probably well suited for these commercial occupations. As your training and experience grow, there is a no definitive career ladder within this career field. However, you will generally work as an inventory, procurement and or vendor manager to become an operations manager, which can all lead to supply chain or logistics management career fields.

EDUCATION AND CERTIFICATION: Minimum of a High School (HS) Diploma or Graduate Record Exam (GRE). The Institute for Supply Management (ISM), Institute of Certified Professional Managers (ICPM), Institute of Hazardous Materials Management (IHMM), Institute of Packaging Professionals (IoPP), and Mail Systems Management Association all provide logistics certifications for veterans interested in getting ahead in the commercial supply career field.

JOB TITLES
Skilled Labor
Administrative Support
Order Processor
Scheduler
Inventory Manager

Procurement Manager (Purchaser)
Vendor Manager
Operations Managers
Warehouse Manager (Supervisor)
Liquid Supply Field Considerations

ROLE: TRANSPORTATION

In today's global economy, drivers and operators are in more demand than ever. All transportation conveyances such as train, trucking, boats, and airplane are needed within the industry. Couriers, freight forwarders and multi-modal transport operators are just some of the many areas for transporters. Generally military transportation workers readily transition into commercial transportation. Therefore, if you desire to continue working as a truck driver, you are probably well suited for commercial occupations. However, if you desire to grow into a managerial position with the transportation career field, there is certainly opportunity for former military Service members. There are usually multiple types of transportation hubs: sea-road, sea-rail and road-rail, and sea-road-rail. With the growth of containerization, intermodal freight transport has become more efficient. Your knowledge, leadership and management skills are needed. Similarly, to the supply section above, as you mature in the career field of transportation management, there is a definitive career ladder for you to follow and can lead to logistics management.

EDUCATION AND CERTIFICATION:

Minimum of a HS Diploma or GRE. If you are considering driving a truck and if you do not already have a Commercial Driver's License (CDL), you must pursue it soon. Other more advanced certifications to assist you in your growth within the commercial transportation career field include: Certified Director of Safety (CDS), Certified Director of Maintenance/Equipment (CDM/E), Certified Safety Supervisor (CSS), Certified Supervisor of Maintenance/Equipment (CSM/E), Certified Driver Trainer (CDT), Certified Cargo Security Professional (CCSP).

OCCUPATIONS

Local Driving
Over the Road / Line Haul Driver
Owner Operator
Lease Purchase Trucking
Scheduler

Intermodal dispatcher
Transportation Manager
Terminal Manager
Transportation Certifications

ROLE: MAINTENANCE

Mechanics are in demand. Even though the job does not pay as well as some sectors, it is steady 9-5 work available everywhere. Veterans that are looking for reliable, stable employment opportunities. Automotive Service Excellence (ASE) certification can give you the keys to a rewarding career. The demand for mechanics and technicians has given thousands of hard working Americans a reliable paycheck.[28] There are many companies where you can find work. Organizations generally perform maintenance on company owned equipment by either organic or third party mechanics. Leasing companies normally maintain their equipment at the leasing facility. However, the leasing company may provide onsite mechanics or contact teams. A good example of the contact team is the maintenance of Material Handling Equipment (MHE) in the warehouse environment.

EDUCATION AND CERTIFICATION:

Minimal of a HS Diploma or GRE. There are numerous certifications available through ASE and National Aviation Academy and Autodesk. This include such certifications as Automobile/Light Truck Diesel Engines, (A9), Drive Train (A3), Suspension and Steering (A4), Heavy Truck Brakes (T4) and Aviation Maintenance Specialist (AMS)

OCCUPATIONS

Automotive Service Technician
Maintenance Supervisor
Maintenance Manager
Fleet Maintenance Manager
AC/HV Technician

Service Mechanic (small machinery and equipment)
Paint and Body Technician
Avionics Technician & Installer
Rail Car Repairman

ROLE: LOGISTICS MANAGEMENT

There are many ways for Combat Arms veterans to enter the logistics management career field. Some will enter commercial logistics management directly from the Service or will obtain a degree in supply chain management. Others will work their way up after gaining experience and increasing their education and certification. However, you will need to document the right blend of skills, experience, education and certification on your resume; thereby translating your capabilities for the hiring official, in terms that they understand. You also need to know your expected entry point into the commercial logistics arena, based upon your experience.

EDUCATION AND CERTIFICATION:

Various. Minimum HS Diploma or GRE. Gaining a Bachelor's or Master's degree in Supply Chain or Logistics Management is a sure-fire way of getting into the Logistics Management Career Field. Great certifications for this role include: Certified Logistics Technician (CLTAE), Certified Production Technician (CPT), Certified in Transportation and Logistics (CTL), Certified Master Logistician (CML), Certified Professional Logistician (CPL), Demonstrated Logistician, Distinguished Logistics Professional (DLP), Global Logistics Associate (GLA), Professional Designation in Logistics and Supply Chain Management (PLS), APICS Certified in Production and Inventory Management (CPIM), APICS Certified Supply Chain Professional (CSCP) APICS Supply Chain Operations Reference Professional (SCOR-P), Certified Fellow in Production and Inventory Management (CFPIM) and of course the PMP Certification.

OCCUPATIONS

Supply Chain Analyst
Logistics Engineer
Logistic Manager
Distribution Manager

IT logistics Manager
Supply Chain Director (Manger)

S6 – Information Technology
Background

Whether commercial, government or military environment, IT service must always deliver confidentiality, integrity, security, and availability. The common IT thread between the military and the commercial world is efficiently and effectively beating the competition. In the military, providing Command, Control, Communications and Computer Systems (C4S) necessary to prevent conflict, respond to crises, and conduct military operations to defeat the enemy is the goal. In the commercial world, the desire is to win business and claim market dominance. In both cases, IT enables the core functions of the business.

However, you must understand the distinctions within commercial IT. In the commercial world, profit is the number one goal. Computers and information systems are not only essential, but will bring business to a halt if they fail. At its core, commercial technology is one of the primary enablers of corporate profit. Therefore, business needs to invest in technology to remain competitive. Since the industrial revolution, companies have consistently desired to out-maneuver their competitors to remain viable and survive. Technology has completely changed the way we do business and is now woven into the fabric of all business efforts. To this end, corporations are constantly seeking additional IT capabilities to streamline business process and increase their competitive advantage. If business operation is the basic building block of business, then IT is the mortar that holds the corporation together. For an in-depth study and analysis of this career field and your many options, should IT be your post career inclination, make sure you read *"The Transitioning Military IT Professional."*

Outlook & Salaries

The outlook for the IT career field is very positive. This field continues to enjoy unfettered global growth with the national average for IT salaries in December of 2015 reporting around $73,080 per year.[29] Further, the outlook for IT employees through 2024 on average

BLS Website:
bls.gov/home.htm

indicates 13 percent growth, far better than the national outlook average of 7 percent.[30] Interestingly, while management positions are faltering in many career fields, computers and information systems managers should expect a 15% growth through 2020, with a median salary over $120,000 per year.[31]

The S6 functions relate closely to the commercial IT as shown from a high level by reviewing Figure 3.9, below. You will find the major roles with their descriptions. Further, specific jobs within each major role are given. An additional way to gain a more in-depth understanding of the IT career field, is by reading *"The Transitioning Military Information Technology Professional"* which is a component of the *"Transitioning Military Series."* When you read this book, you will find much of the research has already been performed for you as you take a deeper dive into commercial IT understanding. For more detailed and up to date information on each role and job listed below, check out the U.S. Department of Labor, BLS website.

INFORMATION TECHNOLOGY

IT is a lucrative career field interwoven into the basic fabric of business. This means that your skills are transportable; you have the ability and opportunity to launch into a lucrative position. You may start out as a technician, but as your management and technological skills develop, you may end up as the CIO, Chief Information Security Officer (CISO) or Chief Operations Officer (COO). With the advent of the Internet of Things (IoT), there is an increasing demand for skilled IT professionals. Technology gives you the ability to perform work from any location, provided you have connectivity. Additionally, the IT field is highly diverse and can take on multiple career paths during a lifetime. Your efforts may contribute to numerous business enhancing capabilities. Your work may improve internal communications support to the company. Finally, cybersecurity is needed for all functions and jobs within IT. As a transitioning Service member, you are fully aware of the criticality in maintaining safety and security in your day-to-day affairs. Commercial technology knows this criticality all too well. If you are inclined to move in the direction of cybersecurity, you may be heavily rewarded for years to come.

ROLE: TELECOM /
NETWORK SERVICES

Due to the onset of Voice Over Internet Protocol (VoIP) technology, there are increasing similarities and blending between the telecommunications and the network career fields. Today there are multiple paths for professionals pursuing the telecommunications and/or network services career field. You may pursue becoming a network services professional or pursue a wireless networking profession. IP technology is the dominant telecommunications method today. In fact, most service members have never worked on anything but VoIP systems. The outlook for the industry is very good, with expectations that the industry will grow to more than $76 billion in 2015.[32]

EDUCATION AND
CERTIFICATION:

Minimum of a HS Diploma. Cisco has forever been at the forefront in network service certification. Cisco offers a great progressive educational and certification program. Juniper Networks, Inc. offers the Juniper Networks Certification Program (JNCP), a multi-tiered program which "validates the Juniper skill set among the world's leading networking professionals."[33] Both Cisco and Juniper Networks offer wireless certification. However, the industry standard for vendor neutral enterprise Wi-Fi certification and training is Certified Wireless Network Professional (CWNP). CWNP offers a specific ladder or progression with certification in Wi-Fi fundamentals, admin, security, analysis, design, expert, and instructor.

OCCUPATIONS

Telecommunications Specialist	Telecom Researcher
Network/VoIP Technician	Network Engineer
Telecommunications Data Technician	Network Administrator
Fiber Technician	Network Architect
Network Operation Center (NOC) Engineer	Network Performance Test Engineer
Mobility / Cellular Network Engineer	Wireless Network Engineer

ROLE: DATA CENTER/ CLOUD SERVICES If your desire is to become a data center professional, there are multiple categories within this IT career field group that you should consider based upon your personality and technical desire. With the advent of cloud computing and desire to reduce cost and complexity within organizations, some companies now subscribe to Data Center as a Service (DCaaS). DCaaS is the provision of offsite physical data center facilities and infrastructure to clients. Clients rent or lease access to the provider's data center using the servers, networking, storage, and other computing resources owned by the DCaaS provider. Security, reliability, speed and availability continue to be the basic essential elements that you must understand and be comfortable administering.

EDUCATION AND CERTIFICATION: Minimum of a HS Diploma. Major players in the field of system administration certification include OS providers like Microsoft, Linux, Red Hat and VMware. Cisco, VMware, Schneider Electric, and the professional association Building Industry Consulting Service International (BICSI) all offer data center management and/ or design certifications. VMware, Citrix, Red Hat, Microsoft, and Cisco all offer virtualization certifications.

OCCUPATIONS

Data Center Technician
IT Systems Administrator /
   Server Administrator
Virtualization Specialist or VMWare
Administrator

Storage Area Network Administrator
Data Center Engineer
Facilities Engineer
Performance Engineer
Cloud Solution Architect

ROLE: APPLICATION / SOFTWARE SUPPORT
Per the BLS, the employment of this career field is projected to grow 17 percent over the next 10 years, which is considerably faster than most occupations. Employment of applications developers is projected to grow at a slightly higher rate (19 percent) while systems developers are projected to grow at 13 percent. Computer software continues to be in demand as the driving factor for this growth. The need for new applications on mobile devices and tablets will help increase the demand for application software developers.[34]

Additionally, the fields of big data, analytics, and business intelligence are in high demand and will continue to see unfettered growth. Everyone entering this career field is expected to have education, basic certification, and some seat time or experience. You must be a writer as the best application and software support personnel must know how to document well.

EDUCATION AND CERTIFICATION:
Most jobs within this career field require bachelor's degrees in computer science or software engineering. Generally, these degree programs have significant math requirements and a software engineering track, where you construct, analyze, and maintain software in a laboratory If you choose to obtain a degree in software engineering, you may want to consider programs that are accredited by ABET, Inc., (abet.org).[35] When desiring to pursue professional software engineering certification, there are two distinguished professional certifications from the professional association known as the Electronics Engineers (IEEE) Computer Society (CS).

OCCUPATIONS

Database Developer / Engineer	App Store Optimization Manager
Front End Developer	Content Manager
Web Developer	Application Developer
Application Developer	Systems Software Developers
Junior Mobile App Developer	Data Warehouse Specialist / Big Data Engineer

ROLE: IT SUPPORT SERVICES

You may desire to become an IT support or help desk manager. A few years ago, the help desk technician or customer support specialist was often viewed as a gateway job into IT as most companies strategically focus on customer satisfaction as a top priority. Today, these trusted individuals play many critical roles in every organization. Other IT support service positions may be more aligned with your personal desires such as content management, Web development, mobile application development, or application store management. With organizations desiring to have a presence on the Internet through some form of social network, you may find a home as a social media manager or a Search Engine Optimization (SEO) manager. Other valuable IT support positions within large organizations include such operations as system license tracking, lifecycle replacement, purchasing, upgrade, and configuration manager. Employment of computer support specialists is projected to grow 12 percent by 2024, faster than the national average. Everyone entering this career field is expected to have basic IT qualifications, good Customer Relation Management (CRM) skills, and know how to document well.

EDUCATION AND CERTIFICATION:

Minimum of a HS Diploma. Great certifications are CompTIA A+, Network + and/or Security + (which is preferred). The Help Desk Institute (HDI) provides low cost certifications to assist in transitioning into a commercial IT support position, such as HDI customer service representative, support center analyst, desktop support technician, and many others. Apple, the non-profit trade association CompTIA and the professional association BICSI all offer certifications in hardware support. If you desire to provide IT support for mobile computing, Cisco, VMware, Citrix and Aruba are renowned premier training and certification organizations. Also, note that the Microsoft Certified Desktop Support Technician (MCDST) is considered an entry level certification.

OCCUPATIONS

Customer Support Representative (Help Desk Technician)
Computer Network Support Specialists
Support Center Analyst / Manager (Help Desk Manager)
IT Service Manager

IT Logistics or Procurement Specialist
Search Engine Optimization (SEO)
Social Media Marketing Manager (SMM)
Digital Marketing Specialist / Manager
Mobile Computing Specialist

ROLE: CYBERSECURITY

Cybersecurity career field should see unprecedented growth by 37% nationwide through 2020. Having a deep specialized related skill set within an IT field such as networking or data-base will increase your capability, your marketability, and enhance your job prospects. Generally, cybersecurity is not an entry-level occupation within the IT industry. Most professionals entering this career field are expected to have significant qualifications and/or certification in either data systems and/or networks.

EDUCATION AND CERTIFICATION:

Minimum of a HS Diploma. Recommended entry certification for those starting out in IT are those like CompTIA's A+ and Network+, individuals working in the cybersecurity field need to have certifications that are more cybersecurity focused, such as Security+. Further, your portfolio of certifications should be robust across several IT fields, prior to delving into the realm of cybersecurity certification. You should consider operating system certifications, Microsoft Certified Solutions Expert (MCSE), Red Hat Certified Technician (RHCT), or Cisco Cybersecurity Specialist (CCS), particularly a Cisco Certified Network Associate (CCNA)-Security.[36] With hackers becoming smarter and more aggressive, Certified Ethical Hacker (CEH) ethical hackers are in high demand.[37] The Certified Information Systems Security (CISSP) from the International Information Systems Security Certification Consortium (ISC)[2] and the Certified Information Security Manager (CISM) from an organization previously known as the Information Systems Audit and Control Association (ISACA) are also recommended cybersecurity certifications.[38] With regard to Business Continuity (BC) and Disaster Recovery (DR), the Disaster Recovery Institute (DRI) International offers the Certified Business Continuity Professional (CBCP). For an in-depth study and analysis of this career field and your many options, read "The Transitioning Military Cybersecurity Professional."

OCCUPATIONS

Forensic Computer Analyst / Computer Crime Investigator	Cybersecurity Specialist
	Intrusion Analyst
Ethical Hacker	Network Security Engineer
Cybersecurity Analyst	Malware Analyst
Threat Analyst	Penetration Tester
Systems Security Architect	Business Continuity Specialist
Vulnerability Analyst/Cybersecurity Tester	Disaster Recovery Specialist

ROLE: IT MANAGEMENT

Military veterans with the desire, experience, and education can transition into the commercial IT management career field. IT management is a demanding and exciting career. If you love and desire to remain around the latest technology and you enjoy working with people, this is the career field for you. IT management not only pays well, but with technology's ever increasing growth, the demand for workers and managers will increase. The Bureau of Labor and Statistics predicts 15% growth for computer and information systems managers from 2012 to 2022, more than twice the national average.[39] IT management can be very interesting as every problem, project, and situation is unique. Most people in IT management would state that the first step into the management career field is project management. This job requires understanding of the IT capabilities and terminology, but does not necessarily demand in-depth knowledge and expertise. This is the position that many military IT managers transition into first after the Service. Your skills at leading teams and your ability to get things done on schedule and to standard make you a great candidate for this career field. Project management is also a great career field with a solid developmental ladder.

EDUCATION AND CERTIFICATION:

If you do not have a degree, get one. Many of the technical experts working for you will have a degree. Beyond that, you should consider obtaining a good entry-level certification in IT management. As mentioned earlier you may want to pursue project management. If so the PMP from PMI is a great way to start. One of your first steps to get the PMP certification is completing the on-line application. As you complete the application, keep in mind that many military activities you led at different levels have direct translation as experience to the project management world. You just need to be able to articulate this information to the reader of your online application. As mentioned previous, "The Transitioning Military Project Manager" is a great resource for further understanding and analysis.

OCCUPATIONS

IT Project Manager	Business Relationship Manager
IT Service Manager	Information Technology Director
IT Program Manager	Chief Information Officer
IT Portfolio Manager	Chief Cybersecurity Officer

Other Methods of Certification
Government Certification

National Defense University

If you are still on active duty and you know you are going to stay in the DoD complex as a civil servant, the National Defense University (NDU) has a very noteworthy certification program. NDU offers certification in the following areas:

NDU Certification
lcollege.ndu.edu

- Logistics
- Cybersecurity
- International Security

Some of these certification programs can lead to a Master of Science (MS) with a concentration in the associated field from NDU. The training is for civil servants, active duty military personnel in the grade of O-4 and above, state and local government employees, as well as the private sector. If you are a DoD civilian, active U.S. Military & Uniformed Services, active Military Reserve or National Guard, you pay no tuition. This is a huge benefit as the cost would be $7,000 – $15,000 for the certifications. Therefore, if you have time prior to transitioning from the military or seeking a civil service position, make sure you take advantage of this very significant benefit. If you are interested in further information, download the iCollege catalog from the NDU homepage.[40]

Defense Acquisition University

If you are still on active duty or already out of the Service, you can obtain free education and certification from the Defense Acquisition University (DAU). Anyone desiring to know more about the acquisition, technology and logistics career fields can take the training, but only civil servants and active duty military can get the certification. The Defense Acquisition Workforce Improvement Act (DAWIA) required the Department of Defense (DoD) to establish a process through which persons in the acquisition workforce would be recognized as

**Information on
DAU Courses:**
dau.mil/default.aspx

having achieved professional status. "Certification is the procedure through which a military Service or DoD Component determines that an employee meets the education, training, and experience standards required for a career level in any acquisition, technology, and logistics career field."[41]

You will need a bachelor's degree to start, but otherwise it is relatively easy to enroll and get the training. There are three levels of DAWIA certification available for DoD civilian employees and military whose career development will include assignment to acquisition-coded positions. While most civil servant positions will not require certifications, job announcements will view this certification as a "quality ranking factor" not a "qualification factor." Therefore, most DoD personnel filling acquisition positions have 24 months to achieve the certification standards (career field/path and level) assigned to the position.

As of the date of this book's publication, Figure 3.10 shows the career field certifications available through DAU, with the IT functional area highlighted in italics.[42]

DAU Career Field Certification Functional Areas

Auditing	Information Technology
Business – Cost Estimating	Life Cycle Logistics
Business – Financial Management	Program Management
Contracting	Production, Quality and Manufacturing
Engineering	Purchasing
Facilities Engineering	Science and Technology Manager
Industrial/Contract Property Management	Test and Evaluation

Figure 3.10 | DAU Career Field Certification Functional Areas

For example, if you want to work within a DoD IT acquisition role, you would need to qualify at DAWIA Level I, II, or III, depending on your position. The requirements for each acquisition career field are specified at the DAU website.[43] By way of example, Figure 3.15 shows the requirements for DAWIA Level I, IT certification:

Core Certification Standards (required for DAWIA certification)	
Information Technology Level I	
Acquisition Training	ACQ 101 Fundamentals of Systems Acquisition Management
Functional Training	ISA 101 Basic Information Systems Acquisition
Education	Formal education not required for certification
Experience	1 year of acquisition experience in information technology

Figure 3.11 | Information Technology Core Certification Standards

The silver lining for DAU certification is two-fold. First, this is high quality, government specific, on-line training that is available to you. Second, this training is available free of charge. If you go the civil service route, this training is essential and will propel your career and significantly enhance your knowledge and skills. While not directly transferrable to the commercial market, certification in these areas can be exploited to support easy and seamless transition. The fact that you have these is proof that you are interested seeking continued career growth.

Education Options

A great way to get into one of the career fields mentioned earlier in the chapter is to use your Post 911 G.I. Bill and obtain a bachelor's degree. Colleges and universities throughout the country offer the following bachelor degrees, with many schools offering associates and master degrees.

There are many veteran friendly colleges and universities. Syracuse University is one such university offering multiple bachelors and masters of science degrees at the Syracuse University.

Syracuse University Veterans Programs:
ischool.syr.edu/academics/
veterans-and-military/
veterans-and-military-
overview

Military Service Training

Each Service offers courses on management. By way of example, make sure to use your Army E-learning benefit prior to getting out. Numerous courses in management exist on this site. Logistics, IT technical training and managerial training are all available. This tremendous benefit, leading to many certifications and degrees, evaporates upon your departure from the Service. Many of these credits are approved by the American Council on Education (ACE).[44]

Army e-Learning Course Catalog:
atrrs.army.mil/selfdevctr/sfcatalog.pdf

Additionally, there are Master of Science and PhD in Computer Science degrees available at the Air Force Institute of Technology (AFIT). The Army School of Information Technology offers advanced training and course works for military and DA civilians. Generally, this education and training will need to be taken as a government employee. If you have the opportunity, take this training prior to your departure from the Service.

Other Training Options

Another way to get desired free training, if you have not yet exited the Service is through the Veterans Career Transition Program (VCTP), provided by Syracuse University and JPMorgan Chase, Inc. These have specified and independent study learning paths with up to six months free online training in such career fields as

VCTP Information
vets.syr.edu/employment/vctp-certification-paths

logistics, IT and project management, leading to certification. Additionally, GR8Transitions4U has other superb books leading to additional great career fields.

Assessment #4 *(Career Field Skills)*

Figure 3.12 is the fourth assessment in the book and explores your personal selection of career field. You may answer the questions here. When you are ready to analyze them, refer to Chapter Five. You can also use the companion guide to this book, available for download at GR8Transitions4U.com. Read each question and choose the correct answer for your current situation.

4: Career Field Skills	Strongly Disagree	Disagree	Neither Agree or Disagree	Agree	Strongly Agree
I am looking at potential career fields and starting to focus on one or two.					
I have pursued certification or degree in my desired career field.					
I have performed work to related to my chosen career field while in the service.					
I am comfortable working with technology and technical people.					
I have studied different occupations within my chosen career field with regard to personal interest.					
I have reviewed different types of certifications and analyzed the best certification for my situation.					
I desire to get an additional certification in an essential area, prior to departing the service.					
I have planned projects or implementations in the military.					
I have performed self preparation and I feel confident in my understanding of commercial functions, services and operations.					
I enjoy the staying abreast of changing commercial environment and advancements within my chosen industry.					

Figure 3.12 | Career Field Skills Assessment

Summary

Once comfortable with your chosen future career path, and your ability to articulate your skills within the commercial market, you will have a competitive advantage when transitioning from the military. The choice to prepare yourself to meet and excel at your post-military career and enjoy the associated career benefits is yours to make. We encourage you to continue your education and learn all you can about your chosen profession and to gain an awareness that transcends job titles, careers and industries. The story below depicts how a Marine, given lemons applied his leadership skills and created lemonade, learning valuable civilian employment skills along the way.

Robert Fry
Military Leadership Application in the Commercial World

*BORN IN ARIZONA, ROBERT FRY GREW UP IN A
BROKEN HOME IN HOUSTON, TEXAS. Even though he
was only in the ninth grade on 9/11, he was so moved, he
decided that he must join the Marine Corps. Three weeks
after high school graduation Robert was standing on the
yellow footprints at Marine Corps Recruit Depot (MCRD) in
San Diego. Just a few short months later, he found himself
in midst of artillery with the 1st Battalion, 11th Marines.
Upon arrival, Robert's unit was preparing for deployment
to Iraq. Somewhat to his surprise, when he arrived in Iraq
at Al Taqaddum, AKA TQ for those familiar, the unit did not
provide fire support. Instead the Marines were employed
as security forces, patrolling and knocking down doors.*

*After a challenging one-year experience, Robert found
his way back safely to the United States and married
his sweetheart who had been with him throughout his
deployment. He was transferred to Keesler Air Force Base,
where he took on an administrative role. The senior NCOs
encouraged him to get an education while at Keesler and
he began to attend community college.*

*He eventually transferred to American Military University
online in pursuit of his bachelor's degree and received
orders to Marine Corps Base Quantico in Virginia. Quantico
was probably not the best place for young Marine. Even
though he was working on his bachelor's degree through
American University, he became somewhat disillusioned as
he was not performing typical Marine Corps duties.*

*Up until his time at Quantico, the Marine Corps had always
taken precedence over his family. Robert had always been
taught and believed his priorities should be first to God,*

second to the Marine Corps, and third to the family. As he embarked on his tour in Quantico, Robert was starting to have second thoughts and he began to realize that his wife and children were extremely important to him. When he started looking at reassignment, the only thing being offered was recruiting. He talked to several NCOs and realized that recruiting duty would be tough on the family. Taking the advice of an older NCO, he talked to his wife about making a joint decision on the recruiting duty. She stated she would support him, but she wanted to take the children and go back home to Texas. Robert agreed to the arrangement and soon missed being with the family, realizing that his family was more important to him than the Marine Corps.

Robert soon finished the bachelor's degree and decided to get out of the Marine Corps. The decision was not easy as Robert loved the Marine Corps and he was concerned about finding a job. All he had ever known since high school was the Marine Corps. The Marine Corps had helped provide for his family and given him an education, while he simultaneously gained management and leadership experience. Robert believed he had everything he needed, but he did not know if it would work out and realized he was just going to have to jump and take a leap of faith.

Robert began his job search, moved to Houston and joined back up with his family. Having gone to the Transition Assistance Program (TAP), he knew he was supposed to start looking early for a job. He flirted with GE Oil in Texas for months. After six interviews, the company was still not ready to offer the job. He applied for another position with St. Luke's Hospital in Houston and received a face-to-face interview within two days. By the time he got to his car after the interview, Robert's phone was ringing and he was being offered a position.

The job was going to pay $20,000 less than Robert's earnings in the Marine Corps. He was disillusioned, as he believed he would make more money than when in the Marines. Robert was contemplating the offer, when the phone rang. It was GE offering him $5000 a year more than St. Luke's. Robert thought about the offer, remembered how long it took GE to make the decision and decided to go with his gut, and stay with the job offer from the hospital. It was a very fortuitous decision. One of the members of the interview panel was formerly in the Navy and became his boss, a great friend and mentor. Even though he was making less money than he desired, his mentor taught Robert healthcare administration, project and business management.

Robert had great experience, education and management capabilities, but he lacked experience in the professional world and industry. It turns out industry experience is extremely valuable and cannot be taught in the Marine Corps. However, military leadership skills are phenomenal once you learn how to apply these to the commercial world and gain commercial industry experience.

Because St. Luke's had a goal of providing the highest quality healthcare. The organization realized that to achieve this goal, they needed to ensure that their people were well educated and current so he was encouraged to get his master's degree. He found St. Luke's to have their arms wide open and is forever grateful to them for being his first commercial job experience. St. Luke's encouraged him to attend a PMI Boot Camp and to get his PMP. He quickly found that even though he was only making $50,000 a year, St Luke's benefits were far superior to many other organizations.

After about two years, St. Luke's was bought by another company and things begin to change drastically. Senior leaders were leaving for various reasons, and soon his mentor left. The politics began to kick in. His mentor called to check up on him several times discussing the situation. Subsequently, Robert's mentor recommended he move to another company.

Robert went to work for a healthcare staffing agency for a couple years where he learned a tremendous amount about the staffing business, candidates and resumes. He found the mission to be very profit focused and that average resume received a seven second look. He also learned that you had to quickly convey your resume to garner hiring manager attention. While he gained a great deal of knowledge in the world of staffing and recruiting, Robert was not happy with the staffing agency and begin to put out feelers for other positions.

Shortly after completing his master's degree in Health Informatics, he was offered an opportunity with Shriners Hospital as a project manager. He has found tremendous satisfaction with this position. Like the Marine Corps, Shriners Hospital has an extraordinary mission. Shriners Hospital is not concerned about trying to increase revenue and keep shareholders happy. Instead their mission is about taking care of children that are very ill with various illnesses, severe burns, or have mobility challenges. Robert now has a fulfilling mission as a project manager for a great organization that does tremendous good for so many children and families. Further, he's been encouraged to get his Lean Six Sigma Black Belt and a certification in healthcare quality.

Robert now knows that when he got out of the Marine Corps, he lacked professional experience. Unfortunately, this is not something the Marine Corps could provide. He thought he would be worth considerably more money on the outside, but now realizes that most will have a challenging time finding a great paying job without commercial experience. Robert's dictum, "When you get out, you're going to take a hit. You've got to work through the suck, but you will end up making more than when you were in the Marines! Remember, you need experience to make money."

The Market Place

**TREMENDOUS OPPORTUNITIES FOR COMBAT ARMS PROFES-
SIONALS ABOUND IN THE COMMERCIAL AND PUBLIC SECTORS.**
The challenge is understanding and making an informed decision about where
to conduct your job search. This very important
decision needs to incorporate your comfort
levels with risk, job satisfaction, security and
growth. Learning about your desires as they
relate to market place characteristics, will give
you a distinct advantage in your job search
decision. You may have already settled on a

> **"Opportunities
> multiply as they
> are seized."**
> ~ Sun Tzu 孫子
> *The Art of War*

target job market. However, if you are unsure, look to this chapter to provide
you with the tools to evaluate the pros and cons of your target market place.

Some transitioning personnel believe they will step into a great paying and
interesting job for the rest of their life, immediately after leaving the Service.
However, this is not typical. Most of us change jobs, companies, and careers
many times. Learning the advantages and disadvantages of multiple transitions can better prepare you and your family.

Opportunities after the military Service fall into roughly three sectors. These sectors are the focus of this chapter: civil service, government contracting, and commercial market place. Even though non-profit organizations are not a focus of this book, a brief discussion of this topic is presented as some Service members choose this path after the Service. For those that enjoy risk and working independently, entrepreneurship is covered briefly. There is a wealth of knowledge readily available on the entrepreneurship market. Like the non-profit organization, entrepreneurship is not a focus as it is beyond the scope and objective of this book.

Check with USA.Gov for a complete list and details of federal benefits. http://usa.gov/Federal-Employees/Benefits.shtml

Each market place is explored regarding environment, opportunity, pay, benefits and career path as they relate to your interest and desires. Options and insights are offered so that you can weigh and consider all facets that impact you the most, from work/life balance to job benefits.

After looking at each sector, the market places are compared within the framework described above. A marketplace assessment is presented to further assist in identifying key factors while determining the best fit for you and your next position. As you read this chapter, note that the terms public sector, government, and civil service are all used interchangeably. Likewise, private sector, commercial company, and corporation are terms used in lieu of commercial market place. DoD contracting is considered a hybrid to these distinct sectors.

Civil Service Market Place

The federal government is the largest employment sector in the nation, hiring nearly 300,000 new employees every year. There are many government departments and agencies. All have many differences, from culture, professional opportunity, and employee satisfaction, and in some cases, pay scales.[1] Generally, civil service provides a tremendous opportunity for those desiring a stable work environment, great benefits and good pay. The reality is that people do not take civil service positions to get wealthy. In general, government workers want to use their skills and make a difference. Therefore, many choose civil service for these reasons, along with a growing number of transitioning military.

"Most candidates interested in working for the government fully understand three clear benefits," said Evan Lesser, co-founder and director of ClearanceJobs. com, a secure website designed to match security-cleared job candidates with top defense industry employers. "First, is the issue of job security. Compared to contractors, Federal agencies are less subject to budget funding shortfalls and cancelled or re-bid contracts. Second, job seekers see a more structured promotion ladder. And third, working for the nation's largest employer means excellent health and retirement benefits."[2] If you are unaware, workers in commercial firms are three times more likely to be fired, compared to federal employees. Civil service positions are generally more stable. This is comforting if stability is one of your most compelling decision factors.

For the complete federal workplace survey:
Bestplacestowork.org/ BPTW/rankings/ governmentwide

Environment

The Partnership for Public Service (PPS), in concert with the audit and financial professional services firm Deloitte, annually publishes the "The Best Places to Work in the Federal Government." This cross-agency assessment provides civil servant's opinions on workplace issues ranging from leadership, WLB, pay and personal ability for innovation.

John Palguta, PPS Vice President of Policy, stated "The reason people go to work for the government is because they want to do something meaningful and make a difference. Civil servants want to make good use of their skills and be engaged in mission accomplishment." The PPS assessment demonstrates civil servant personal job satisfaction and overall organization satisfaction.[3] An important factor making up organization satisfaction is pay. The last couple of years have been difficult for civil servant salary increases. Not surprisingly, recent reports show a significant categorical drop in satisfaction of federal pay, due to the political and economic environment. Potentially due to fiscal concerns, there was also a decline in training and development opportunities, and rewards and advancement.[4]

Additionally, assessment results are broken into federal agency size categories. Not surprisingly, the Departments of Navy, Air Force and Army are all listed and considered large agencies with 15,000 or more employees. Interestingly, for the civil servants interviewed, National Aeronautics and Space Administration finished on top with the highest satisfaction, and the Department of Homeland Security finished last. Figure 4.1 provides statistical results in overall job satisfaction for all large Federal agencies. No sector receives a perfect score of 100, but the higher the score, indicates greater personal job satisfaction within that agency.

RANK	LARGE AGENCY (15,000 OR MORE EMPLOYEES)	SCORE
1	National Aeronautics and Space Administration	74
2	Department of Commerce	67.6
3	Intelligence Community	67.3
4	Department of State	65.6
5	Department of Justice	63.58
6	Social Security Administration	63
7	Department of Health and Human Services	61.9
8	Department of Transportation	60.9
9	Department of the Treasury	59.5
10	Environmental Protection Agency (tie)	59.3
10	Department of the Navy (tie)	59.3
12	Department of the Interior	58.9
13	Department of Veterans Affairs	57.3
14	Department of the Air Force	57.2
15	Office of the Secretary of Defense, Joint Staff, Defense Agencies	57
16	Department of Agriculture	56.1
17	Department of Labor (tie)	55.6
17	Department of the Army (tie)	55.6
19	Department of Homeland Security	46.8

Figure 4.1 | Statistical Results for Job Satisfaction – Large Agency

Opportunity

Generally, civil service positions provide tremendous opportunities for military members in transition. The federal government gives you an advantage due to your veteran status. Having served in a war, having a military connected disability or having served on active

Civil Service Job Site:
http://USAJOBS.GOV

duty all give you an advantage and put you in different competitive categories. Therefore, your military Service provides a significant benefit when competing for high quality civil service positions.

AUTHORITY	PROVISION	WHO IT APPLIES TO
VRA	VRA allows appointment of eligible Veterans up to the GS-11 or equivalent grade level.	• Disabled Veterans • Veterans who served on active duty in the Armed Forces during a war declared by Congress, or in a campaign or expedition for which a campaign badge has been authorized. • Veterans who, while serving on active duty in the Armed Forces, participated in a military operation for which the Armed Forces Service Medal (AFSM) was awarded • Veterans separated from active duty within the past 3 years.
30% Disabled	Enables a hiring manager to appoint an eligible candidate to any position for which he or she is qualified, without competition. Unlike the VRA, there is no grade-level limitation.	• Disabled Veterans who were retired from active military service with a service-connected disability rating of 30 percent or more • Disabled Veterans rated by the Department of Veterans Affairs (VA) as having a compensable service-connected disability of 30 percent or more.
VEOA	Gives preference eligible and certain eligible Veterans' access to jobs that otherwise only would have been available to status employees.	• Preference eligible • Service personnel separated after 3 or more years of continuous active service performed under honorable conditions.

Figure 4.2 | Civil Service Hiring Authorities for Veterans

When applying for civil service positions, you need to understand how the job announcement enables or precludes your advantageous veteran status. In many civil service applications, veteran status is awarded extra 'points' when identified by the applicant. You may be eligible to compete under one or more categories designed for veterans such as Veterans' Recruitment Appointment (VRA), 30 Percent or More Disabled Veterans, and Veterans Employment Opportunities Act of 1998 (VEOA). These special hiring authorities for veterans give you a significant advantage if you are qualified. Figure 4.2 summarizes these hiring authorities:

Remember, your competition when applying for these positions are current Federal employees with status and other United States citizens. Therefore, understanding your veteran eligibility is critical. Also, be aware that your eligibility does not make you qualified for the position. You may be eligible under a special hiring authority, but you may not be qualified based on your experience or education.

Information on veterans transitioning to civil service:
http://fedshirevets.gov/hire/hm/shav/

The difference between eligibility and qualifications can be summed up as follows. Qualification is based solely on your KSAs, and education, as discussed in chapters two and three. Eligibility is meeting one or more criteria such as disabled veteran. A recent dimension in determining qualification for a job is the use of self-assessments, which are now becoming more of a standard than the exception. A series of questions are asked of the candidate during the application process to determine if you meet the KSAs for the position. Civil service hiring is also based on your capability to demonstrate your experience at the next lower level. So, if you are applying for a GS 12, your resume and questionnaire answers need to demonstrate your competencies and experience at the GS 11 level. Therefore, if you do not demonstrate your qualification for the position, your

Information on answering federal self-assessments:
http://govcentral.monster.com/benefits/articles/2370-best-ways-to-answer-federal-self-assessments

documentation will not be forwarded to the hiring official for review. Further information on answering federal self-assessments can be found on monster. com.

Like other market places, there are significant advantages when it comes to mobility or being able to move to serve the needs of the government. When finding a position in a different locality you may receive pay for a move much like that in the military. Every position on USAJOBS.gov will tell you if relocation is authorized. Sometimes, the department will offer relocation if it is hard to find someone with certain qualifications and/or interest in going to that particular location. For example, finding a job with relocation to the Washington, D.C. area can be difficult. However, most rural locations without a significant local applicant pool will often provide relocation and/or financial incentive.

The best method for applying for civil service positions is through the comprehensive website "USAJOBS.gov." This website not only posts jobs available by title description and location, it allows you to apply and track your application status. Helpful resume and application tips are given, enabling you to put your best foot forward.

Pay

GS Pay Tables:
http://opm.gov/policy-data-oversight/pay-leave/salaries-wages/2015/general-schedule

Pay is a subject that is of great interest to all of us. Government Service (GS) pay scales operate on grade levels and geography. GS pay tables are standardized much like military pay tables, with the addition of locality pay adjustments. In 2014, a GS-14, Manager in San Francisco can earn an annual salary of $115,613 to $150,291 depending on step. While in Tampa, the same position pays from $97,657 to $126,249. An entry level GS-12 Project Manager can earn $69,497 in Salt Lake City, and about $6,000 a year more in the Washington, D.C. area. Therefore, you should look at the correct scale for the location for which you are applying. As an example, Tampa has no special "locality pay area" table. In the case where there is no scale for the metropolitan area you are considering, look at the scale called "Rest of United States." Figure 4.3 below delineates the GS Pay Scale for the San Francisco (35.5% locality payment) area. Remember, no locality pay is given in overseas areas. Instead, overseas employees receive Cost of Living Allowance (COLA).

SALARY TABLE 20
INCORPORATING THE 1% GENERAL SCHEDULE INCRE
FOR THE LOCALITY PAY AREA OF SAN JOSE-S
TOTAL INCREASE
EFFECTIVE JANUA

Annual Rates by Grade

Grade	Step 1	Step 2	Step 3	Step 4	Step 5	Ste
1	$ 24,301	$ 25,114	$ 25,922	$ 26,726	$ 27,534	$ 28
2	27,323	27,973	28,878	29,644	29,975	30
3	29,811	30,805	31,798	32,791	33,785	3
4	33,467	34,582	35,697	36,812	37,927	39,0
5	37,443	38,692	39,941	41,190	42,438	43,6
6	41,738	43,129	44,520	45,910	47,301	

Figure 4.3 | Salary Table 2014-SF, Locality Pay for San Francisco

Benefits

A tremendous number of benefits are available to civil servants. Benefits are organized into five major categories: benefits and insurance, leave and WLB, pay and savings, retirement, and personnel records. There is some variety between agencies, and the country's economy plays a great role in the availability of some benefits such as education. The major benefit categories are listed in Figure 4.4, but there are many benefits in each category. A complete detailed list is available at each agency Web site and at usa.gov/Federal-Employees/Benefits.shtml. Remember, not all benefits are available from each department or agency.

Civil Servant Benefits:
usa.gov/Federal-Employees/Benefits.shtml

HIGH LEVEL BENEFITS FOR CIVIL SERVANTS
Benefits and Insurance Programs
Leave and Work-Life Balance
Pay and Savings Plans
Retirement
Personnel Records

Figure 4.4| Civil Service Benefits [5]

DoD Contracting Market Place

Many believe that the DoD contracting life blends the best of both attributes of GS and commercial market place while staying in a career supporting the military. The DoD contract environment is different from your military experience. You are still ultimately working for the defense of the nation, but you serve two masters. More importantly, the risk and rewards are both potentially greater than that of the civil service.

As a DoD contractor, you remain engaged with the defense of our nation. Many Service members want to spend their post-military career doing something that feels familiar, and comfortable. This is why many pursue DoD contracting after military Service. Transitioning to a DoD contracting position gives you comfort of a familiar language, and a grasp on the needs of the mission and organization.[6]

Environment

For many, DoD contracting is a very appealing post-military career. In addition to potentially better wages for your work efforts than civil service, you have the potential to stay within the same department or agency you already know and understand while receiving significant flexibility not previously enjoyed. In most locations, you have the right to move on to another position or company should you become weary of your contract situation, bosses attitude, or government leadership. This knowledge and understanding provides relief for many in difficult or challenging situations.

Understanding the associated risks of DoD contracting is also very important. First, some find the government-contractor relationship challenging, especially after having been on the government side for a long period. If you choose to remain in the DoD environment, never loose site of the fact that the contractual relationship is adversarial by its very nature. There is goodness in this adversarial relationship. It is not only good for the taxpayer, but also provides constant checks and balances for both sides. The desire is to have a harmonious environment, with equilibrium between government over-watch and contract performance. If either side gains the upper hand, then a difficult and challenging work environment will exist.

> *One of the most important but difficult tasks in contract administration is to develop a proper working relationship. Cooperation between the parties is essential if the work is to be successfully performed, and yet the parties are, in a very real sense, adversaries. The Government often attempts to obtain performance within the contract price, while the contractor attempts to maximize profits either by doing the minimum acceptable work or by attempting to obtain price increase.[7]*

Why is this information important to you? Understanding the contract and government relationship is essential to your day-to-day life as a contractor. The question you face is how to deal with these types of relationship issues. Do you enjoy working through these types of challenges with contract leaders, program managers, and associated government counterparts? It is important to find the right fit. Learning to understand the challenges that lie ahead and being prepared to identify them, process them, and create optional courses of action will help you be successful. Examples of challenges you will face as a DoD contractor are summarized below.

One of the first things you should reconcile as a new contractor is that most contracts have an estimated date for completion. This proves challenging for most military veterans, as your term of Service was relatively guaranteed. How to deal with uncertainty of follow on work with your contract can be challenging and stressful. This is potentially the contractor's greatest anxiety. Not only does the contractor have to perform well, satisfy the customer, accomplish the tasks on time and to standard, but he or she must be keenly aware of the remaining contract duration and how well the contract at large is performing.

If you desire a steady income, you may find coping with this risk difficult. The contractors that feel most comfortable with this arrangement will typically grow a sizable rainy day fund (2-3 months' salary) to assist during contract transitional periods. This risk mitigation strategy will provide some peace of mind,

especially in these challenging economic and ever changing political times. Always remember, that even in a down economy, the government remains the largest single employer in the country and there are plenty of contracting jobs available, especially if you are willing to relocate.

Another challenge to reconcile with is that you will be working with either a military or a civil servant government lead. They will have the final say on decisions. Constrained by rules and regulations, the federal government is not famous for innovation or speed of bureaucratic consensus. These challenges may feel stifling or even frustrate some into choosing to move on to another occupation.

Opportunity

Like civil service, federal contractors receive similar benefits regarding mobility, future work and security. Contracts extend well beyond Washington, D.C., with departments, agencies and offices around the world. That makes finding a job for those seeking a specific location, or desiring an opportunity to change localities, a great potential benefit. If you are mobile and good at what you do, the contract industry is going to have a job for you.[8] People move from job to job as contracts come and go. A DoD contracting career offers a significant chance for mobility and professional growth.[9]

Professional diversity is an added benefit of being a DoD contractor. As you acquire a variety of experience, you will be increasingly sought after. You will have a chance to move in and out of various professional experiences. If you are already an expert in one area, working different tasks and functions means you will have the chance to develop new skills and explore potential new specialized areas.

Finally, like civil service, your security clearance is invaluable if you choose to stay in DoD contracting. If your clearance re-investigation date has passed and you have lost your clearance, but you have the experience needed, many contractors will offer to recapture your clearance as part of your hiring package. Additionally, many federal contractors will offer 'upgrades' of your clearance for required positions to meet certain contract requirements. You will not necessarily be reminded of your periodic investigation dates, so stay on top of your clearance. If a life event occurs such as financial issues, divorce, or arrest, make sure you inform your security officer quickly.

Job availability, good starting salaries and promotion potential are all positive aspects of contracting if you can go to where the jobs are. A defense contracting career is often the preference of many. If you have the skills wanted by the contractor at the right time, they will hire you on the spot with minimal paperwork and put you to work immediately. Further, you will have more control of your own destiny as your performance is the driving force in your career path. If you are performing, you will be promoted. If you are dissatisfied, then you can move to a more demanding job opportunity offering better pay.

Pay

As a contractor, you have a greater ability to negotiate a salary than your civil servant counter parts. As a company competes for new work with the government, a proposal is developed outlining various positions on the contract. The company will bid a specified price that considers a pay band for each position. Once awarded, the program manager has some flexibility within the

Negotiating Salary?
See Appendix B or:
GR8Transitions4u.com

pay band when hiring employees. This information may allow you to negotiate salary within the pay band for your desired position. Therefore, you must request a salary within a position's pay band, or you will probably not be hired.

As in the earlier quote from Sun Tzu, it is obvious the greatest road to success is to know yourself and know your environment. It is often said the first party to mention a figure during salary negotiation will not fare as well in the negotiation. Therefore, when questioned about your salary requirements, it is best to ask about the pay band for your position and request a well thought out number that resides within that pay band. Appendix D of this book provides a method for determining a realistic salary request.

Benefits

First, know that HR organizations will have specialists and experts that will explain and share current offerings in line with Federal and state laws. Generally, there is minimal variation between contract companies when it comes to benefit packages. Regardless of which Federal contractor you work for, you will find 100-150 hours offered as Paid Time Off (PTO) annually; or stated in military terms, leave. Of interest is that you accrue and take PTO by the hour and not by the day. This is helpful as you will need to take PTO occasionally for doctors' appointments, sick leave, or vacation. Unfortunately, most of the appointments that you are used to going to during a military duty day should be charged as PTO. Another option, if available, is flex time. Many companies desire that you get 40 hours of work in one week or 80 hours over a two-week period. Often, you can flex hours within the pay period so that you could work 42 hours one week and 38 the next. This type of arrangement varies by company. Regardless, just remember that the time cards are archived for inspection by the Defense Contract Audit Agency (DCAA). Therefore, contract and personal integrity are on the line and the time card must accurately reflect hours worked.

With regards to health benefits, most companies offer comprehensive healthcare where you pay a share and the company pays a share. If you are a retiree, some companies adjust your salary if you utilize your retiree healthcare benefit. Just know, if you desire to use a company's healthcare you can, but there will more than likely be a deduction from your pay check for the benefit. Vision and dental are shared benefits as well. Just like your health insurance, if you are using TRICARE as an example, this benefit may not be of interest to you.

A flexible spending account is often available by larger companies in which you place some of your salary into an account for healthcare related expenditures. The dollars you place in this program reduce your taxable income, but must all be used for healthcare by the end of each year. Most companies, big and small will offer a 401(k) plan for long-term retirement savings. These plans will generally be matching funds up to about 3-5%. The company will determine which investment group you will be buying into and you will generally have a choice of funds. Some companies allow all your dollars to be fully "vested" upon your initial investment. Others will allow you to have their matching funds after a vesting period has surpassed (i.e., 50% vested after 2 years, 100% after 3 years). These vesting periods vary considerably between companies. Just remember that the 401(k) is for long term retirement savings and significant penalties will normally be applied if you take out money prior to age 59½[10]. Additionally, some companies offer different types of stock options at discounted rates. This is an inexpensive way to invest in your company as you avoid brokerage fees in addition to any discount offered. Regardless, it is always recommended to place enough money in the 401(k) to get the matching funds, as you do not want to leave money on the table.

Larger companies have educational, training and certification assistance. Training authorization typically requires justification for the position you are in. Generally, companies will ask that you sign a document stating that you will not leave the company for some period (often 1 year) after taking the training dollars. This needs to be considered prior to taking training if you are thinking about changing companies, because some will hold back your last pay check to pay for your training if you have not completed the allotted time.

If you have not surmised, bigger DoD contract companies generally offer bigger and better benefits. The alternative is that smaller companies may have greater salary and might be more attractive to employees desiring fewer benefits. Therefore, if benefits are not that important and more pay is a consideration, you may consider going to work for a smaller company. For example, if you have retiree benefits, you could negotiate more in salary. Finally, some small companies have greater flexibility for profit sharing with their employees. Regardless, weigh all the benefits, salary, profit sharing and bonus capabilities to find the total compensation of the position. This exercise will assist you in weighing your options when comparing multiple job offers.

Commercial Market Place

Transitioning into the commercial market place from the military requires considerable risk tolerance and a high level of confidence in your ability to perform in a competitive environment. As mentioned at the beginning of this chapter, workers in commercial firms are three times more likely to be fired as compared to federal employees. Working in the commercial market is not for the faint of heart, and the risks must be managed. However, most working in the commercial market quickly state that the rewards for this risk outweigh the job security of civil service.

Environment

Because workers strive for personal growth and reward, the commercial environment is often very competitive. In the commercial environment, employees generally try to remain competitive through innovation and providing business value to the organization. This determination and drive often require numerous man hours above and beyond a traditional 40-hour work week. Understandably, most workers join the commercial market place to earn significant amount of money, to be trained or gain experience, positioning themselves to earn significant money later.

It is always the desire in commercial market to achieve profitability and make money. Maximizing profit will drive all business decisions. If there are two choices, the best business case will be selected. Companies and managers will consistently pursue the highest potential profit at the best value every time they make a business decision. What this means to you as a potential worker in the commercial environment is that you must understand this concept and remain viable to the company, otherwise your services will not be needed for long. The profit concept is foreign to most public-sector workers, including Service members. Be advised, this concept sometimes becomes a bias against hiring veterans for some commercial hiring managers.

In high performing companies, there is tremendous focus on the bottom line. Managers desire to achieve this focus which leads to well understood, top to bottom goals and objectives. Two most important objectives driving decision making in the commercial market place are solution and price. Focusing on solution and price typically drives satisfaction and value in the commercial market. Managers must focus on providing and creating added value through the products and services offered by their company. The best solution is sought, as it increases ROI and profit. Therefore, you need to be synchronized with management as you are held accountable for your work, and you are rewarded for success and potentially fired for failure.[11]

You need to understand what drives value in your work environment. Knowing this will help you align your day-to-day work effort as you deal with the customer as well as connect better when looking for a job. Nothing is more nerve racking than going to an interview or giving a presentation and not understanding how your employer perceives or derives value. Further, you are far better off talking to your leadership about their view regarding the best solution and profit, rather than unfinanced requirements and perceived cost savings which do not aid the organization's bottom line.

Opportunity

The commercial sector is set apart from the public sector regarding rapid personal growth potential for achievers with financial reward and the promise of a creative and innovative environment. Rapid change is pervasive with the ever-changing business environment, and you will be rewarded if you embrace and become part of the change. One of the great attributes associated with the commercial market place is that your high performance will enable you to progress quickly without regard to a pay scale or longevity. As you work on your professional goals and career path, utilize opportunities to gain additional and diverse experience. Seek out ways to gain internal qualifications through training that aligns with your career goals. Keep in mind where you want to be and take on challenges to posture yourself for future success.

Financial reward is based largely on your ability to remain viable and valuable to the organization. If you are adding to the bottom line you will be rewarded financially. The company rewards your positive impact and participation because if you move on, it may lose profit and key knowledge to the competition.

Innovation and creativity are also well rewarded in the private sector, if the innovation aids to the company's competitiveness, market position, or bottom line.

Remember, to remain competitive, companies will seek innovative workers and it will make change based on the business environment. If you like an exciting and dynamic environment, the commercial sector is for you.

Pay

Conventional wisdom has it that you'll always make more money in the commercial market place, with lower pay being the trade-off for job security in the Federal government.

That's generally true. The Federal Salary Council, a group of union officials and pay policy experts, says federal workers overall earn about 35 percent less than their commercial-sector peers.[12]

Benefits

In general, benefits are similar or better than DoD contracting. The one exception is small business as, you may have fewer benefits. Small businesses must offer the following benefits as they are considered mandatory by the federal government.[13]

- Time off to vote, serve on a jury and perform military Service.
- Comply with all workers' compensation requirements.

- Withhold FICA taxes from employees' paychecks and pay your own portion of FICA taxes, providing employees with retirement and disability benefits.

- Pay state and federal unemployment taxes, thus providing benefits for unemployed workers.

- Contribute to state short-term disability programs in states where such programs exist.

- Comply with the Federal Family and Medical Leave (FMLA).

Surprisingly, the following benefits are not required to be given to employees and you may see a variation of these benefits at every company.

- Retirement plans

- Health plans (most employers are still working to distinguish the various options of the Affordable Care Act)

- Dental or vision plans

- Life insurance plans

- Paid vacations, holidays or sick leave

Having said all of this, most large companies offer tremendous benefits and some unexpected surprises upon arrival. Price Waterhouse Coopers (PWC)[14] advertises the following "Perks" on its website:

- **Sabbatical:** Employees can take four-week sabbaticals with 20 percent to 50 percent of pay.

- **Tuition Reimbursement and Scholarships:** Employees can get up to $5,250 in financial assistance to further their education.

- **401(k):** PWC contributes 5 percent of an employees' annual pay to their 401(k) retirement savings plans even if they don't make their own contribution.

- **Volunteer Hours:** Every employee receives 10 hours per year of paid time off to volunteer for charities of their choice.

- **Rewards and Recognitions:** Employees can earn contribution awards when managers or partners recognize them for excellence, outstanding effort and team work.

Non-Profit Organizations - FFRDC/UARC

A Nonprofit Organization (NPO) functions with a purpose or function, other than making a profit. NPOs are typically dedicated to furthering a social cause or advocating ideals.

FFRDC are unique nonprofit entities sponsored and funded by the U.S. government. The Federal Acquisition Regulation (FAR) requires they operate in the public interest free from organizational conflicts of interest and can therefore assist in ways that industry contractors cannot. FFRDCs assist with governmental scientific research and analysis, systems development, and systems acquisition. FFRDCs operate in the industries of defense, homeland security, energy, aviation, space, health and human services, and tax administration. FFRDCs are grouped into three categories focusing on different types of activities:

- System engineering and integration centers
- Study and analysis centers
- Research and development centers (includes national laboratories)

FFRDCs were established to provide the DoD with unique analytical, engineering, and research capabilities in many areas where the government cannot attract and retain personnel in sufficient depth and numbers. Currently, there are over 40 recognized FFRDCs sponsored by the U.S. government. University Affiliated Research Centers (UARC) are strategic DoD research centers associated with one or more universities.

If you decide to go this route, an NPO wants to know that you are truly interested in their cause and what they are doing – just as much as the skills that you have. You may show your loyalty to the cause and your interest by starting out with the organization as a volunteer.

Interested in FFRDC or UARC?
defenseinnovation
marketplace.mil/FFRDC_
UARC.html

Entrepreneurship

As mentioned earlier in the chapter, the subject of entrepreneurship is only lightly discussed. There are many resources available for this sector as there are many variations of start-up businesses. For example, you might want to start a supply or transportation company or consulting firm as a disabled veteran or minority owned business. You may decide that you desire to become an owner/operator of your own truck.

Regardless, each city/county/state offers a variety of classes and seminars on how to successfully start these types of companies. If you should try entrepreneurship as a consultant or business, keep in mind the following concepts.

- You must be willing to take on risk to achieve success.
- There is no cook book and you cannot be a quitter.
- You need to have deep pockets or backing.
- Need to understand the business, tax and government laws, contracting associated with the business you are going pursuing.
- The measure of success for entrepreneurship is survivability 5 to 10 years out.
- Entrepreneurship is tough on the family and quality of life, unless there are other sources of income.
- You must be an optimist and pride yourself on doing things differently.

Market Place Comparison

Understanding how the commercial market place differs from the government is essential for your success in transitioning from the military. Knowing the value proposition is essential. Public organizations will perceive value through mission accomplishment with the least amount of hassle or disturbance. Private organizations will find value through seeking out the least cost and greatest capability, thereby enhancing the bottom line.

When looking at this question from the employee perspective, a term coined in England when comparing the public and private market place is "Sector Envy."

Universally, it appears that the "Grass is always greener" when looking at the opposing market place. With wildly varying risks, rewards, salaries, benefits and job security, "Sector Envy" is a very appropriate term among American workers as well. Let's compare the public and private market place as they relate to your personal desires.

"Sector Envy" it is interesting to note that there is an increase in the migration of workers moving back and forth between government agencies, DoD contractors and the commercial market place. Employees with contracting backgrounds make easy transitions into federal and civil servant jobs due to their skills, knowledge and abilities (SKAs). Generally, as a former Service member becomes more familiar with commercial certifications and the new environment, they become more marketable in the commercial market place. Know that many have come before you and not only changed jobs, but also market places on multiple occasions.

So, what do you need to know? You should be aware that there are many factors that separate public and private sectors. Fundamental environmental factors include: value proposition, business case, turnover challenges, and measures of success. Obvious factors are financial rewards, job security, benefits, and your ability to easily transition from the Service. Some of the not so obvious factors are WLB, changing work environment, workload and career ladder. A few comparative environmental factors are given below:

Value proposition - Private sector managers worry about creating added value, while public-sector managers are often stifled by outdated, restrictive laws, regulations and policies that prevent rapid change or action.

Business case - In private industry there are clear well understood top to bottom goals and objectives. In the public-sector goals are often divergent or disparate and can lead to confusion.

Turnover challenges - In government, leaders are often rotated in and out to ensure proper grooming and development of leadership. This rotation of leadership creates potential organizational change based on personality rather than achieving unity of movement towards goals and objectives. The corollary in the business world is a business merger or hostile takeover.

Key Performance Indicators (PKI) – In the absence of clearly understood business goals, government often invents measures of success that might be more aligned to short-term contractual and personal goals versus long-term business goals.

Stone walling – In the government setting, if a leader is not well received, senior civil servants will slow roll and wait out leadership change. This is especially true for political appointees or temporary military leadership. In the private sector, there is no business case for this type of activity, as most companies will find this unacceptable.

These fundamental factors have huge environmental implications on workplace satisfaction. Figure 4.5 below compares positive responses from federal government employees against commercial-sector workers. These questions reflect the impact of some environmental factors previously discussed. The results show the public sector holds a slight edge over the commercial market place when employees are asked if they like the kind of work they do.[15] However,

QUESTION	GOVERNMENT - WIDE	COMMERCIAL MARKET PLACE	GAP
I like the kind of work I do.	81.2	75.0	6.2
My work gives me a feeling of personal accomplishment.	69.7	70.0	-0.3
I have enough information to do my job well.	69.3	71.0	-1.7
The people I work with cooperate to get the job done.	72.3	78.0	-5.7
I am given a real opportunity to improve my skills in my organization.	59.6	66.0	-6.4
Overall, how good a job do you feel is being done by your immediate supervisor/ team leader?	65.8	73.0	-7.2
How satisfied are you with your opportunity to get a better job in your organization?	31.5	44.0	-12.5
How satisfied are you with the training you receive for your present job?	46.6	61.0	-14.4
How satisfied are you with the information you receive from management on what's going on in your organization?	44.8	60.0	-15.2
How satisfied are you with the recognition you receive for doing a good job?	42.6	64.0	- 21.4

Figure 4.5 | Comparison - Federal to Commercial Work Satisfaction

when it comes to recognition, training and supervisors, the commercial market place employees are a big winner.

Personal Market Place Satisfaction Scale

Having read the environmental factors, a side by side Market Place Satisfaction Scale is presented for your understanding of the remaining factor differences. When looking at the market places for future opportunities, it is beneficial to optimize your search. Most of us do not have the latitude of time on our side to look for and, more importantly get a job. You can spend months searching through the job listings. We spend much of our lives at work, and it is worth being happy during that time. Additionally, about 20% of people leave their jobs every year, according to the BLS.

If it is important for you not to be part of the statistic and continually rotate jobs, there are a few items to consider. A key consideration to staying in a particular job is your personal satisfaction. Sometimes we forget the "personal satisfaction" factor, as this will increase the chances of remaining in the same position. Make an honest evaluation and list the factors necessary for your workdays to be as enjoyable and rewarding as possible.

Nine satisfaction elements are utilized in the personal satisfaction scale. The definition of each element used in this tool is defined below in Figure 4.6.

ELEMENT	DEFINITION
Creative Environment	Opportunity/need to be creative in the job.
Financial Reward	Probability of salary increase and bonus based on success.
Change	Frequency of change expected on the job to maintain position.
Workload	Level of work expected to perform on the job to sustain position.
Career Ladder	Clearly defined job growth expectations and requirements.
Education Reimbursement	Financial reimbursement for additional education and certification.
Work/Life Balance	Based on rules and work week expectations, presents a level of work/life balance important to keep personnel satisfied.
Job Risk	Volatility and chance of losing your job due to issues outside of your control.
Benefits	Level of standardized benefits to include medical/dental, savings, retirement, vacation time, education, etc.
Ease of Transition	Determination of transitional ease for former service member.

Figure 4.6 | Factor Definitions

145

To assist in your organization of these personal satisfaction elements, the following market place satisfaction scale is presented. The columns represent the four market places covered in this chapter: Civil Service, DoD Contractor, Commercial, Non-Profits and Entrepreneur. The rows represent typical elements as they relate to the market place. The scale is presented below in Figure 4.9. Probabilities are plotted for each factor in each marketplace based upon whether the element has a high-medium-low likelihood of influence in the marketplace. Data for the grid is based upon years of discussion and experience. There will always be exceptions, but for your purposes, the table should prove helpful to those in transition from the military, offering a foundation that can be customized based upon your own experiences.

At a glance, two items that might be of importance to you are security and work/life balance. If these two are important to you, you may gravitate towards the civil service work. If you enjoy risk and desire a highly competitive and potentially creative environment, you may align yourself with commercial industry, or perhaps, even entrepreneurship.

When considering all the elements of the table, you will notice that the civil service marketplace offers more stability and you can have relative confidence that you will be able to remain in the position, with a standard offering of benefits, salary and a pro-active work/life balance. If you desire to climb the corporate ladder while creating an opportunity of accelerated promotions and achieve a better than average salary due to your creative mindset, you will be better served in either the commercial or entrepreneurial markets.

Finally, the scale roughly correlates with personality types. You may have previously identified with either 'Type A' or 'Type B' behaviors. 'Type A' personalities are typically ambitious, rigidly *organized,* high achieving, *"workaholics,"* multi-taskers, highly motivated, insist on deadlines, and hate both delays and ambivalence.

Contrastingly, 'Type B' personalities live at a lower stress level and typically work steadily, enjoying achievement but do not become stressed if immediate gratification is not present. They may be creative and enjoy exploring ideas and concepts and are often reflective.

Use Figure 4.7 to assist you in developing thoughts on which market place may provide the best landing space for you after the Service based on your personality and style. Take a few moments and ponder the difference to ensure you are pursuing the best match for your lifestyle.

Personal Market Place Satisfaction Scale

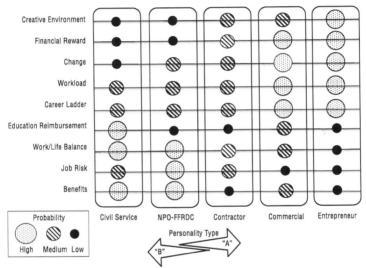

Figure 4.7 | Personal Market Place Satisfaction

Assessment #5 *(Market Place)*

Figure 4.8 is the fifth and final assessment in the book, exploring personal factors that influence which market place offers the best alignment to your interests. You may answer the assessment questions here. When you are ready to analyze them, refer to Chapter 5. You can also utilize the companion guide to this book, available for download and print out on-line at GR8Transitions4U.com. Read each question and choose the correct answer for your current situation.

5: MARKET PLACE

	Strongly Disagree	Disagree	Neither Agree OR Disagree	Agree	Strongly Agree
Potential salary increase is more important to me than job security.					
A potentially stressful work place and long hours are not concerns for me.					
Creativity and innovation are more important than procedures.					
I am excited by the prospect of leaving public service and trying something different in the private sector.					
I desire promotions based on personal performance rather than on pay scales and longevity.					
Switching companies or changing positions frequently are not concerns for me.					
Feeling safe from competition and losing my job are factors I rarely think about.					
I desire to work in an environment that rewards my innovative behavior and 'out of the box' thinking.					
An environment where I can share and use my military experiences and knowledge is not overly important to me.					
I prefer driving or "making" my career path rather than waiting on promotion.					

Figure 4.8 | Market Place Assessment

Summary

Once comfortable with the basics, knowledge of the market place will help you gain a competitive advantage and keep you from proceeding down the wrong path for your next career. A few parting thoughts are presented as you progress in your job search and transition:

1. If you have a target market place in mind, make sure your resume is tailored to the markets you desire and that your network and connections will be able to assist.

2. You can inquire and ask questions at the end of an interview such as how the company views different positions; how risk adverse the company is; how mature their documentation processes are; what tools are used; what career path options are open to someone starting in your position and what criteria is used to measure and advance.

3. Once at the job, think out-of-the-box. Do not just go into the job and expect a list of daily activities to perform. In the military, you had to adapt. Now is the time to utilize that trait.

4. Gain confidence in the new position by understanding both the official and unofficial political fabric of your environment.

5. Understand your peers and your boss. As you master your expected job skills, continue to branch out as far as possible to other divisions, groups, and teams. This knowledge will increase your overall understanding and appreciation of the organization, as a holistic view will assist you in evaluating the position you are in and how it connects with your expectations and goals.

The choice to prepare yourself and perform good market place selection, is yours to make. You are encouraged to continue to grow your understanding of these different sectors. You may find yourself trying out multiple market places during your career. In the story below, discover how a former Special Operator transitioned from combat operations, to defense contractor and then finding fulfillment as a successful entrepreneur.

Evan Hafer
Revolutionary

BORN IN MOSCOW, IDAHO, EVAN GREW UP STRONG AND WITH A PATRIOT'S HEART. Raised by his father; with chores, hunting, fishing, and school, there was little time for play. Graduating from Lewiston High School, Evan aspired to become a Navy Seal. However, an older gentleman told him that his goal of becoming a Seal was flawed and he should seriously consider going Army Special Operations.

Evan began his military journey, attending Infantry Basic Training shortly after graduating high school. He joined the Idaho National Guard and started the Simultaneous Membership Program (SMP) at the University of Idaho in Moscow. Continuing to pursue his aspirations of becoming Special Forces (SF), Evan chose not to go to ROTC Advanced Camp between his junior and senior year; and instead attended the first phase of the Special Forces Qualification Course, or the Special Forces Assessment and Selection (SFAS).

Evan graduated from the Special Forces Qualification Course (SFQC) in 2000. One year later, while standing in the middle of a swamp at the Joint Readiness Training Center (JRTC), Evan learned about the attacks of 911. Within a few weeks, Evan was in the Philippines, on to Kuwait and then Iraq. During the next couple of years, with complete commitment to the war effort, Evan returned to the United States for only two weeks.

Maintaining several parallel jobs with the National Guard, CIA and the State Department, Evan found himself continuously in Iraq and Afghanistan until 2011. Excitement and the belief in the bigger picture enabled Evan to sustain his efforts during these challenging years. After a total of 5 solid years of deployment in the wilds of Afghanistan and Iraq, Evan took a job teaching for the CIA back in the U.S. During this job, he became disenchanted with vacillating government foreign policy and decided to make a professional change.

Evan begin thinking about settling down and getting married. Even though he had thought about getting married earlier on, he never desired to build a family while in deployment status. Evan had experience first-hand how difficult marriage was on so many of his SF brothers, especially having to bury a few of them with young children and brides.

Believing he was through with his deployments, Evan married and the couple were soon expecting a child. Needing money for his new family, while still maintaining a sense of adventure; Evan jumped into the world of entrepreneurship.

Evan's first attempt at creating a company was Twist Rate, a crowd funding business which helped veterans with great ideas, gain patent and funding. Twist Rate was not dissimilar from Kickstarter, but was dedicated to helping veterans. This was a natural progression, as Evan was now beginning his life's journey and passion, helping other warriors. He had decided to become an entrepreneur in the military space, because so many guys and gals had great ideas but little to no business experience. Evan quickly learned that he could not run a business halfway. He had to step away from the military world and dedicate everything to the business.

Jeff Kirkham and he were business partners with similar traits and thoughts about their military experience and their business. But by 2014, after dedicating heart and soul into the business, Evan realized he did not know enough about business to be successful. After 18 months Evan shut Twist Rate down. He found a business mentor name is Jayson Ortiz, of Lexington Law, the predecessor to Credit Repair. Jayson began to mentor Evan and Jeff, and they learned volumes about the business. Shortly thereafter, they created their second startup company, Readyman, providing products and education.

To make ends meet, Evan had started The Black Rifle Coffee Company (BRCC) a few months earlier. Because he could not afford a brick-and-mortar store, he began to grind coffee at night and sell it online through web sites he had built. Evan quickly found he was working more hours than ever anytime previously, in his life. Jayson had taught him the business concepts necessary to run a successful company, but the rest was Evan's pure energy and a desire to succeed. He was now throwing all his energy at the startup companies.

The concept behind BRCC was to create a high-end coffee shop for gun owners and conservatives to hang out and have discussions, as an alternative to other more liberal coffee shops. As he only made $20,000 over 18 months and to keep things together financially, Evan sold two houses with his wife; one in Denver and one in Seattle. Working 20 hours a day seven days a week Evan stated that he was not going to lose. He would grind coffee all night, perform customer service, pack and ship boxes, learn HTML code and continue to modify and hone his *web site. During the day, he worked other jobs to try and survive. With gratitude, he kept reminding himself that no one was shooting at him and he need not be concerned about losing his legs to and IED.*

He believed in himself and knew he could make it; it was just going to take time. Evan found this to be the most excruciatingly difficult thing he had ever done in his life. He was reinventing himself at 37 years old. Evan slept most nights at the office, stating "This time was particularly challenging, with a new child and wife," who he saw for just a few minutes every week.

Today, many folks say Evan is doing well and beginning to reap the rewards. Recently on Fox News, Evan boldly stated that he would hire 10,000 veterans, making it clear that he will never give up his desire to help veterans. In a revolutionary tone, he desires to "emancipate" military personnel and put them to work with good commercial jobs, as they have willing sacrificed so much for their country. On entrepreneurship, Evan shamelessly states, "There is no secret, you need to roll up your sleeves and go to work." Evan knows that owning your own business is a great option for those that have the right mindset. Entrepreneurship is exhilarating and it takes the right kind of person, with tremendous fortitude.

The Right Fit

NOW IT IS YOUR TURN.

While reading this book, you have gained focus of your strengths, simultaneously learning about your potential in the commercial job market. You have the logic behind positioning yourself for the job market and you have gained

the confidence to attack the competition. Now you will organize these elements together to shift your mental posture from the defensive to the offensive.

> *"One defends when his strength is inadequate; he attacks when it is abundant."*
>
> ~Sun Tzu 孫子
> *The Art of War*

Combining the knowledge gained from this book with the personal information you collected through the assessments will facilitate the creation of a high impact personal strategic roadmap. This exciting instrument provides directed self-awareness while gaining an understanding of your strengths and the confidence required taking on the next challenge.

Several tools are introduced in this chapter. The first tool is for charting your assessment scores collected in earlier chapters. This tool identifies those personal areas that can be exploited (strengths) and those areas for possible improvement. The second tool is the Personal Strategic Roadmap. Assessment scores that reflect areas for possible improvement will be transferred onto your personal strategic roadmap. This roadmap will be used continuously as you track, monitor, and achieve your personal goals.

To gain the best results, work through the process with honest introspection and reflection. Completing these steps enables your preference for market place, career and level of readiness for transitioning into the commercial market. There are three steps involved:

1. Gaining an understanding and control of personal information and capabilities that you have, thereby reducing risks of the unknown.

2. Analyzing outcomes of each assessment to identify what you already possess in your "kit bag" for successful resume writing, interviewing, and transition.

3. Setting goals based on those areas you choose for improvement. These improvements are to be charted, monitored, and tracked on the Personal Strategic Roadmap until they are achieved.

Step One - Gaining Control of Your Personal Information (The UNK-UNK Chart)

In certain areas of the military and commercial world, the UNK-UNK chart is used to depict information available about organizations. The title of the UNK-UNK chart is derived from using "UNK" as an abbreviation to "Unknown." The chart is useful not only to military planning and operation groups, but to commercial organizations performing risk analysis. When you transform an organizational construct to a personal perspective, the UNK-UNK chart is useful in identifying and understanding what you know and don't know about yourself.

The UNK-UNK chart is broken into four quadrants (Figure 5.1). Quadrants are defined with regard to the terms "Known" and "Unknown." These terms refer to a general understanding of information an organization has awareness of ("knowns") and information not known ("unknowns"). When you array these two terms on both sides of the chart and step through the following analysis, an approach to reducing your "unknowns" begins to unfold. Organizations categorize information as follows: What information they know (KK); what they know that they don't know (KU); what they do not know that they know (UK); and what information they do not know exists and are completely unaware of (UU).

The upper left quadrant (KK-information you know you know) is a very valuable commodity. In this quadrant, the organization is "self-aware" and this knowledge can be exploited. By way of a military example, if you know you know the location of the enemy, you plan and move to contact to destroy the enemy at this location. Similarly, in business, a corporation would want to try to exploit its capabilities in the marketplace if they knew they had a competitive advantage. From a personal perspective, your skills, characteristics, abilities, and sense for the type of marketplace you want to pursue are very valuable. Acknowledge and exploit this information on your resume and during your interviews to achieve the best career alignment.

The upper right quadrant (KU, or, know what you do not know) denotes an organization, which understands they do not have certain information elements needed for success. Capturing these information elements provides tremendous value for study, assessment and improvement within the organization. For example, if a company does not have market information they consider valuable, they work to resolve the information shortfall

UNK-UNK Chart		
	Known	**Unknown**
Known	KK	KU
Unknown	UK	UU

Figure 5.1 | UNK-UNK Chart

to gain a competitive advantage. From a personal perspective, knowing that you do not have a capability is of vital importance. During an interview, not knowing the hiring manager's expectations and how the organization perceives value can bring the interview process to a halt. Take some time to know the customer to try and reduce the risk associated with this quadrant. KU elements become goals for your Personal Strategic Roadmap. Achieving these associated goals turn KUs into KKs, increasing your competitive edge.

The bottom left quadrants (UK, or, you don't know what you know), is very harmful in combat. To avoid this outcome, military organizations employ a term or slogan "Who else needs to know?" When critical information is not shared, it can cause mission failure. A company may know they have a capability, but fail to see its value or how to exploit the capability, and their competitor gets to market faster. Applying this quadrant to your personal transition, you want to ensure you have uncovered your capabilities, even the ones that you do not expect to be of significant marketability. During interviews, take time to exploit and share your accomplishments, certifications, and experiences as they relate to the company.

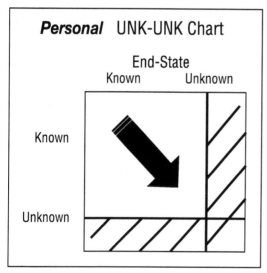

Figure 5.2 | Competitive Gain

Finally, the bottom right quadrant (UU, or information you don't know that you don't know) is all about reaction. "Ignorance is bliss" is a common cliché associated with this quadrant. In this quadrant, action occurs and change happens rapidly if you do not have the information necessary for counter-action. It is the riskiest of quadrants as there are unexpected outcomes, because you could not anticipate events. In the corporate world, while you continue the status quo, your competitor may develop something viable and exploit the market opportunity before you ever realize what happened!

Why go through the exercise of analyzing the UNK-UNK chart? Your objective is to reduce the size of any unknowns and associated risks. As shown in Figure 5.2, reducing the level of "unexpected unknowns" and turning them into "knowns" is the best method to increase your personal edge and confidence. There will always be "unknown" shortcomings, but it is essential to reduce the 'unknown' quadrant as much as possible by expanding other quadrants, making your 'known' area as large as possible. For this to happen, reflect upon your undiscovered skills and characteristics.

With the knowledge of the UNK-UNK chart, let us use the remaining tools of this book to help you determine what areas you need to exploit and what you need to improve upon.

Step Two - Understanding Assessment Results

Analyzing assessment outcomes assists in determining what you already have in your "kit bag" for transitional success. In each prior chapter, assessments were provided in five key transitional areas, summarized in Figure 5.3 below. As mentioned in the introduction, your assessment results should have been documented in the gem formats, available through the free downloadable companion guide found at Gr8Transitions4u.com.

Assessment Type	Chapter	Topic Areas
Personal Environmental	2	Family, re-locations, financial obligations, retirement objectives, schools, faith, etc.
Timing (already to transition)	2	Service goals met, training/certification goals, time remaining, commitment, health, choice/force, financial preparedness
Characteristics/Abilities	2	Risk type, leadership, motivation, creativity, managing others, personal growth, organizational skills, repeatability, working with others, visionary
Skills	3	Military skills, educations, certifications, credentials, jobs
Market Place	4	Civil Service, contractor (DoD), commercial market places analyzed based upon: income, stress competition, predictability, longevity, mental growth, benefits, commitment

Figure 5.2 | Competitive Gain

Star Charting

To assess your strengths and improvement areas, a chart in the form of a star will be created utilizing the companion guide. Begin building the star by charting each assessment score on a 'gem' (Figure 5.4) on the y-axis. The y-axis represents your readiness to transition; or how 'ready' you are to transition from the military. For each assessment, use the question number and plot answer results on the gem axis. It is highly recommended that you use the free companion guide for the assessment. However, the five gems and the star can be manually recreated.

When plotting the results of your assessments, you will likely find more than one answer on an axis point. Simply cluster the plotted points. Analysis of each assessment gem offers a journey to unfolding your personal roadmap. In turn, the roadmap will guide you to the best-suited career path in the best-suited market place.

SCORING: Using question #, plot answer on axis

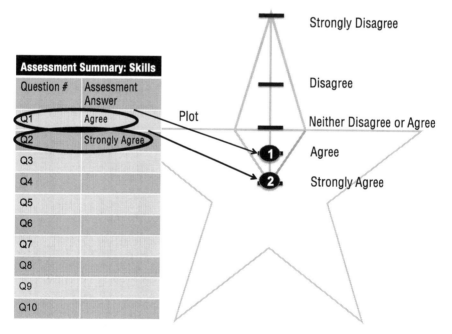

Figure 5.4 | Star Chart Mapping

Once each gem is completed, combine all gems with the associated assessment results to build the Star Chart provided in the companion guide to view your aggregate results (Figure 5.5). When combined, these plotted assessment results form the shape of a star, resulting in a personal index. Your personal index summarizes key indicators from your personal, environmental, timing, marketplace and skills assessments; clearly stating your readiness, marketplace, and ease of transition from the military. With this knowledge, you will understand the best options to pursue, given your strategy goals and objectives.

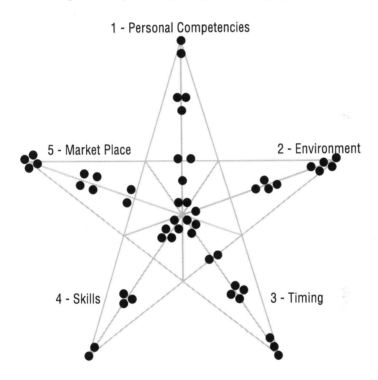

Figure 5.5 | Star Chart Assessment Results

Within the star is the shape of a pentagon (Figure 5.6). Assessment answers plotted within the pentagon represent your strengths. These strengths must be captured and are items to be exploited in your job search and interviews. Assessment answers plotted outside of the pentagon suggest that these are potential areas important to improve, and to be transferred to your Personal

Strategic Roadmap discussed in Step Three, below. Once the analysis of your assessment answers has been completed, you are ready to move on to creating your personal strategic roadmap.

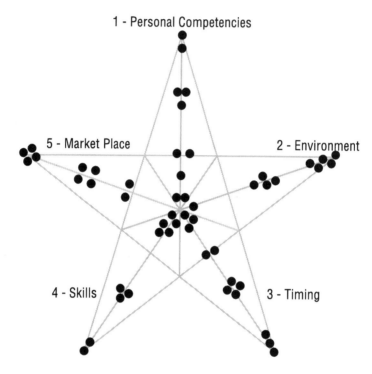

Figure 5.6 | Star Chart Areas for Improvement and Exploitation

Step Three - Setting your Goals

Next, use the Personal Strategic Roadmap to capture your noted areas of improvement from the assessments and increase your probability of transition success. The outcome of this step will be the Personal Strategic Roadmap shown in Appendix C. A full size, editable Personal Strategic Roadmap is also available in the free online companion guide. There are four main sections to the roadmap as shown in Figure 5.7.

> "The real opportunity for success lies within the person, and not the job."
>
> ~ Zig Ziglar

Personal Strategic Roadmap Sections	
1.	Improvements
2.	Vision
3.	Goals and Success
4.	Commit and Attest

Figure 5.7 | Strategic Roadmap Improvements

Use the Personal Strategic Roadmap to list your goals and establish how you will achieve these goals, along with setting the target timeframes for each goal. It is on your roadmap that you will track and monitor these goals until achieved. You will need to monitor your goals on a recurring basis and track your progress. As goals are met, reward yourself, remove each of them from the roadmap and transfer each of these goals to your resume or exploit during your next interview.

Follow the next repeatable actions to complete each critical section of the roadmap and gain the full benefit.

a. Section 1 - **Capture Improvements:** As mentioned in Step 2, identify all assessment answers outside of the pentagon. Transfer these improvements to the top portion of the roadmap in the improvements section. It is important to capture all improvements from all assessments. For example, plotted results from the Skills Assessment Gem determine a need to achieve a commercial certification. In the improvements section of the Personal Strategic Road Map, list those items in part 4, *skills* as shown in Figure 5.8 below:

Figure 5.8 | Strategic Map Improvements

b. Section 2 - **State Your Personal Vision:** Based upon your reading and the improvements captured from Section 1, reflect upon how you desire to work on these improvements. Some of the improvements might be independent of others, such as your interest to take a class to achieve a certification. Some improvements might be best combined with others. For example, you may desire to focus your job search in the civil service market place and geographically target your job search to the Northeast region of the United States where you can be close to a major airport. To adequately capture the influences in achieving your personal vision, write what you want to achieve with the qualifiers that are important to you in the vision section. Include some or all the following: Job place/location (overseas country or state, city), timeframe, market-

> "I actually think most people don't want Google to answer their questions. They want Google to tell them what they should be doing next."
>
> ~ Eric Schmidt, Google CEO

place focus, salary range, possible positions, risk level you are willing to take, industries, and any other considerations. An example is given in Figure 5.9 below:

VISION: Based upon your reading and the five assessment areas above, restate your job objectives to include some or all of the following: Job place/location (CONUS/OCONUS, state/city, timeframe, marketplace focus, salary range, possible positions, risk level you are willing to take, industries, and any other considerations.
YOUR VISION: Make myself marketable for a commercial cybersecurity career, in the civil service market place in the southeastern region of the U.S., with a major airport nearby. By early 2018, I want my resume to reflect my credentials and all my IT experience.

Figure 5.9 | Strategic Map Vision

c. Section 3 - **Create Goals and identify Success:** Now you will create goals from your areas of improvement. If there are more than four improvements, it is recommended that you focus on three or four most important to you. Further, take into consideration the level of effort and time associated with the success of achieving the goal. Some improvement/goals might be independent of one another, such as your interest to take a class to achieve a certification. Some improvement/goals might be best grouped with one or more improvements to clarify and better define success. Transform your improvements into goals that can be achieved with an identified timeframe and measured. For example, transform the improvement 'get a certification' to the goal of 'Cisco Certified Network Associate Routing & Switching (CCNA)'. Post the steps you need to take to achieve the goal, as well as a specific timeframe that you want to achieve the goal as shown in Figure 5.10 below.

GOALS: Pick most important improvement areas from above you want to focus on, depending on level of complexity, learning, or duration (i.e., school).
*List: goals, align which Assessment it ties, year/quarter/month expected to achieve, and present your achievement path (how you will get to your goal and possible

PRIORITY	GOAL STATEMENT	ASSESSMENT TIE	PATH TO ACHIEVING GOAL	YEAR/QTR/MO TO ACHIEVE (personally set)				ACHIEVED?
GOAL #1	CISSP Certification	__ Environment __ Characteristics __ Timing __ Skills __ Market Place	I will research classes available free of charge from military and other organizations, study, apply for certification, take the exam and pass!	03-2015 Class	04-2015 Application	01-2016 Take Exam	Update Resume with New Cert	YES / NO Reschedule or no longer need Date ____
GOAL #2		__ Environment __ Characteristics __ Timing __ Skills __ Market Place						YES / NO Reschedule or no longer need Date ____
GOAL #3		__ Environment __ Characteristics __ Timing __ Skills __ Market Place						YES / NO Reschedule or no longer need Date ____
GOAL #4		__ Environment __ Characteristics __ Timing __ Skills __ Market Place						YES / NO Reschedule or no longer need Date ____

Figure 5.10 | Strategic Map Goals and Achievement

Set a reminder through your calendar to review your progress on each goal listed. Depending on the urgency of the goal, review your roadmap weekly. Do this religiously and do not falter. Look at your roadmap and ask yourself – "What progress or steps have I taken to move towards achieving this goal?" Once progress is achieved, make notes in the 'Path to Achieving Goal' column. If there are outside circumstances that have caused a slip to the right of your scheduled achievement – annotate and move on. Ask yourself, "Was it a slip based upon not working to achieve the goal, or an outside circumstance that was out of your control?" Assess the situation and adjust your goal schedule accordingly in the 'Year/Quarter/Month to Achieve' area. If you achieve the goal – mark 'yes' and celebrate! You are that much closer to an easier and successful transition.

d. **Commit and Attest:** Once you identify what you want to do, annotate it, then sign and date the roadmap as shown in Figure 5.11 below. If you have a family member or a mentor you want to watch and monitor with you, get them to co-sign. Why? You need to remind yourself and your family that you are committed to achieving these goals and that you want to remain accountable. Make a copy of this form and hang it on your refrigerator, or keep it in your wallet. Set a repeatable time for a thorough review of your personal strategic roadmap, preferably with the co-signer and revisit the courses of actions if necessary.

> *"Seeing your goals written in ink on paper will have a powerful effect on your mind."*
> ~ Anonymous

While this is a roadmap that captures the steps you need to transition from the military, the goals themselves are not cast in stone. If for some reason a goal becomes overcome by events, do not see this as a failure. Carefully assess the situation and the circumstances surrounding the reason why the goal is not achievable and take it off the list. Revisit Sections A through D and transform other improvement areas as they develop into goals. Through achieving these goals, you will increase your 'knowns', thereby increasing your opportunity for job transition and success.

Summary

In this chapter, you gain an understanding of your strengths and weaknesses as identified in the assessments provided earlier in the book. These weaknesses are marked for improvement and are translated into goals and annotated in the Personal Strategic Roadmap. Your strengths become areas to highlight on a resume and in an interview.

The bottom line is to increase your "knowns" and reduce the risk of the "unknowns" through preparation, planning and analysis. The more assessment results within the pentagon, the higher probability that you are ready to transition with minimum issues and stress. Use your strategic roadmap to achieve areas of improvement. This actionable exercise will increase the probability of success as you look and interview for jobs in the right market place that best fits you!

Many external resources, models, examples and anecdotes are provided for your consideration throughout this book. It is up to you to select and use the tools that best fit your situation. Transitioning from the military is never easy, but if you can find some nuggets within this book that you can use, then the book will have fulfilled its purpose. Finally, just know you are not alone. Many have come before you and have made the transition. Draw upon others to assist you with their transitional stories through GR8Transitions4U.com. Just like the case study below, keep fighting the good fight and you will be successful in the next exciting phase of your life – plan on it!

Joe Hacia -
You Ain't Good Enough!

GROWING UP AS AN ARMY BRAT AND SON OF AN INFANTRY MAJOR, JOE HACIA DID NOT HAVE TO LOOK FAR FOR TROUBLE. In fact, trouble found him on multiple occasions. His hijinks and lack of discipline eventually landed him at Lyman Ward Military Academy in southern Alabama for his seventh-grade year of school. A few years later, after an additional series of personal challenges, Joe was given the ultimatum to straighten up or join the Service. This was an easy choice for Joe, as he had always wanted to be an Army Ranger.

After basic training and the infantry school, Joe was assigned to a mechanized infantry company in the Big Red One. Joe mentioned to leadership that he wanted to go to a Ranger Battalion. He had already hit a few bumps in the road, and he was told that he would never be good enough to be a Ranger. This is not the first-time Joe had been told he was not good enough. However, his discipline and determination made him push harder. Not long after, Joe began to accelerate within the unit and he eventually obtained a slot and attended Airborne School. He was assigned to the 1/75th Ranger Battalion, where he attended Ranger school, Scuba school, Pathfinder school, became a jump master, and was subsequently involved with combat operations in Grenada.

During the next few years, Joe would serve as a Ranger Instructor, get married and knock out an associate's degree. He was subsequently transferred to the Joint Readiness Training Center (JRTC), where he began the push for his desire to become a pilot. Joe submitted a warrant officer packet and was promptly told by leadership that he would never be a warrant officer, and especially a pilot. Once again, he refused to listen to the criticism and dug deeper. Working hard to get there, Joe was eventually accepted to Warrant Officer Candidate School, with a few more knocks and bangs along the way. He was placed in a leadership position and had a misunderstanding with one of the other candidates. Joe was recycled but eventually finished in the top of the class at flight school, selecting the bird of his choice.

Joe's first flight assignment was with a medical evacuation company at Fort Polk, Louisiana. As he learned about the company being re-organized and sent to Fort Bragg where he did not want to go, he decided it was time to apply for a pilot position with the 160th Special Operations Aviation Regiment (SOAR). He was initially excepted, but later told he needed more experience. So, Joe volunteered to go to Korea to get more flight experience. Once again he was discouraged, but not down and out.

After Korea, he attended the maintenance manager's test pilot course at Fort Eustis and was reassigned to Fort Bragg. He was told at Fort Bragg that as a maintenance test pilot he was not going to be able to fly missions, which he desperately desired and needed the hours to be accepted into the 160th SOAR. Once again Joe could've been discouraged, instead he put together a plan to be a test pilot and a mission pilot simultaneously, which was not typical at the time.

After three years at Fort Bragg, Joe was finally accepted into the 160th SOAR. Joe constantly flew dangerous night combat missions in Afghanistan and Iraq over the next few years. Doing extremely well with the SOAR as a mission and test pilot, Joe became a flight leader in just three years which typically would take five; which some never obtain. After flying 100s of nighttime special operation combat missions with the 160th SOAR for over 10 years, it became apparent Joe needed to attend to his dying father. The network he had developed through years of exposure to the Rangers and the 160th enable him to find a position at United States Special Operations Command (USSOCOM) near his father's home.

Joe eventually retired and found a civil service position at MacDill through his network. However, always concerned about his career and hearing the echoes in his head of "You ain't good enough" and perceiving that his career had plateaued, he decided to start back to school to get his bachelor's degree in business. He had decided earlier that he wanted to work in business someday and he had figured out that he had enough GI Bill dollars left to work on an MBA. Even though he subsequently has been promoted within civil service, Joe desires to move outside government to the corporate business world once he finishes the MBA.

Joe is very thankful for his military experience. It allowed him to grow and do things he never imagined as a troubled young boy. One of the greatest lessons learned for Joe, "When told you cannot do something or that you are not good enough, let it become a motivator and hit the accelerator." When you come up against obstacles, rather than have a negative attitude, present yourself in a manner to get on the obstacle and over the hurdle.

Appendix

Appendix A – Certifications & License

As discussed earlier in the book, some occupations require certification, education or license. Further, other occupations may require some or all of these. This appendix provides a list containing certifications and license by career field. Additionally, the supporting certifying organization is included. This is not a comprehensive list, but does provide a method for thinking about certifications that may be of interest to you. In fact, many jobs may have multiple certifications or certifying bodies, as many certifications are specialized. Every attempt has been made to provide the most recognizable occupational certifications.

A special note on IT certifications. There are two methods for developing a certification portfolio. If you go deep and become highly specialized in a single area, you become desirable as a subject matter expert. However, if you go wide and take certifications that cross multiple sectors, your flexibility and adaptability to fit into multiple career paths will provide insurance for jobs. These certifications are recommended by multiple IT information and advocacy groups such as Tom's IT Pro, Global Knowledge® and CNET®.

If you are considering a license, understand that most of the license listed below are managed separately by state or local government. There is significant variation between geographic localities and states when looking at requirements and qualifiers. Therefore, it is essential to review the governing body's requirements for the license.

	Certification/License	Resource
PERSONNEL	Professional in Human Resources (PHR)	hrci.org/our-programs/our-certifications/phr
	Senior Professional in Human Resources® (SPHR®)	hrci.org/our-programs/our-certifications/sphr
	International Foundation of Employee Benefit Plans (IFEBP)	ifebp.org/
	National Association of Legal Assistants (NALA) Certified Paralegal	nala.org/certification/exam-application-and-qualifications
	Hubspot Inbound	certification.hubspot.com/inbound-certification
	Google Analytics	support.google.com/partners/answer/6089738?hl=en
	Google AdWords	support.google.com/partners/answer/3154326?hl=en
INTELLIGENCE AND SECURITY	National Contract Management Association (NCMA)	ncmahq.org/learn-and-advance/certification
	Defense Acquisition Workforce Improvement Act (DAWIA)	icatalog.dau.mil/onlinecatalog/CareerLvl.aspx
	Insurance licensure (varies by state)	study.com/insurance_agent_certification.html
	Professional Business Analyst (PBA)	pmi.org/certifications/types/business-analysis-pba
	Certified Business Analysis Professional™ (CBAP®)	iiba.org/Certification-Recognition/certification levels.aspx
	Oracle Business Intelligence Certification	education.oracle.com/pls/web_prod-plq-dad/db_pages.getpage?page_id=458&get_params=p_track_id - OBIFS11gOPN
	SAS Business Intelligence Certifications	support.sas.com/certify/creds/sba.html
	Certified Business Intelligence Professional (CBIP)	tdwi.org/cbip
	Home Inspection Certification Associates (ICA)	icaschool.com/
	Private Investigator license (Varies by State)	privateinvestigatoredu.org/license-requirements/
	Certified Management Consultant (CMC)	imcusa.org/?page=CERTIFICATION
	Lean Six Sigma	6sigma.us
	Certified E-Marketing Analyst	icecc.com/certifications.html
OPERATIONS AND TRAINING	Project Management Professional®	pmi.org/Certification/Project-Management-Professional-PMP.aspx
	Project +®	certification.comptia.org/certifications/project
	Program Management Certification®	pmi.org/certification/program-management-professional-pgmp.aspx
	Lean Six Sigma	6sigma.us
	ACF - American Culinary Federation certification	acfchefs.org/ACF/Certify/AboutCertification/CertificationSummary/ACF/Certify/About/Summary
	Culinary Arts Certificate	chefs.edu/programs/le-cordon-bleu-culinary-arts-program/certificate-in-le-cordon-bleu-culinary-arts
	Certified Hotel Administrator (CHA®)	ahlei.org/Products/Certifications/Certified-Hotel-Administrator-(CHA%C2%AE)/
	Hospitality Management Certificate	phoenix.edu/programs/continuing-education/certificate-programs/business-and-management/cert-hpm.html

	Certification/License	Resource
OPERATIONS AND TRAINING	Designing Learning Certificate - Association for Talent Development	td.org/Education/Programs/Designing-Learning-Certificate
	Certified Public Relations Specialist (CPRS)	publicrelationscertificate.com/
	OPMP - Operations & Performance Management Professional	ashrae.org/education-certification/certification/opmp-operations-and-performance-management-professional-certification
	CPSP - Certified Professional Sales Person	nasp.com
	CMMP - Certified Marketing Management Professional	theiimp.org/cmmp-designatio
LOGISTICS	Certified Supply Chain Professional (CSCP)	apics.org/careers-education-professional-development/certification/cscp
	Certified in Production and Inventory Management (CPIM)	apics.org/careers-education-professional-development/certification/cpim
	Certified Professional in Supply Management (CPSM)	instituteforsupplymanagement.org/certification/content.cfm?ItemNumber=30150&navItemNumber=30182
	Certified Professional in Supplier Diversity (CPSD)	instituteforsupplymanagement.org/certification/content.cfm?ItemNumber=30150&navItemNumber=30182
	SCPro™ Council of Supply Chain Management Professionals (CSCMP)	cscmp.org/CSCMP/Certification/SCPro_Certification_Overview/CSCMP/Certify/SCPro__Certification_Overview.aspx
	CDL - Commercial Drivers License (varies by state)	dmv.org/apply-cdl.php
	American Society for Quality (ASQ)	asq.org
	American Society of Transportation and Logistics, Inc. (AST&L)	astl.org
	APICS The Association for Operations Management	apics.org
	Automotive Service Excellence (ASE)	ase.com
	Computing Technology Industry Association (CompTIA)	comptia.org
	In-Plant Printing and Mailing Association	ipma.org
	Institute for Supply Management (ISM)	comptia.org
	Institute of Certified Professional Managers (ICPM)	instituteforsupplymanagement.org
	Institute of Hazardous Materials Management (IHMM)	ihmm.org
	Institute of Packaging Professionals (IoPP)	iopp.org
	Mail Systems Management Association	msmanational.org
	Manufacturing Skill Standards Council (MSSC)	msscusa.org
	Professional Evaluation and Certification Board (PECB)	pecb.org
	Society for Maintenance and Reliability Professionals (SMRP)	smrp.org
	The International Society of Logistics (SOLE)	sole.org
	Universal Public Procurement Certification Council (UPPCC)	uppcc.org

Certification/License	Resource
iNARTE Telecommunications Engineer	inarte.org/certifications/inarte-telecommunications-certification/
Certified Telecommunications Network Specialist (CTNS)	teracomtraining.com
Certified IP Telecom Network Specialist (CIPTS)	teracomtraining.com
Registered Communications Distribution Designer (RCDD)	bicsi.org/double.aspx?l=2558&r=2560
Certified in Convergent Network Technologies (CCNT)	ccntonline.com/article/ccnt-certification-3.asp
Cisco Certified Network Professional (CCNP) certifications/ccnp-collaboration	learningnetwork.cisco.com/community/
Microsoft Certified Solutions Expert (MCSE)	microsoft.com/learning/en-us/mcse-certification.aspx
Linux Professional Institute Certifications (LPIC)	lpi.org/linux-certifications
Red Hat Certified Engineer (RHCE)	redhat.com/training/certifications/rhce/
VCP6-DCV - VMware Certified Professional 6 - Data Center Virtualization	mylearn.vmware.com/mgrReg/plan.cfm?plan=64178&ui=www_cert#tab-requirements
CompTIA Server+	certification.comptia.org/getCertified/certifications/server.aspx
Cisco Certified Network Professional (CCNP) Data Center	cisco.com/web/learning/certifications/professional/ccnp_datacenter/index.html
VMware Certified Professional 6 - Data Center Virtualization (VCP6-DCV)	mylearn.vmware.com/mgrReg/plan.cfm?plan=64178&ui=www_cert#tab-requirements
Schneider Electric Data Center Certified Associate (DCCA)	www2.schneider-electric.com/sites/corporate/en/products-services/training/energy-university/data-center-certificate-program.page
BICSI Data Center Design Consultant (DCDC)	bicsi.org/double.aspx?l=5194&r=5620
VMware Virtualization Certifications	mylearn.vmware.com/mgrReg/plan.cfm?plan=64178&ui=www_cert
Citrix Virtualization Certifications	training.citrix.com/cms/index.php/certification/virtualization/
Red Hat Certified Virtualization Administrator (RHCVA)	redhat.com/training/certifications/rhcva
Cisco Unified Computing Specialist Certifications	cisco.com/web/learning/certifications/specialist/dc/uc_design.html
Private Cloud (MCSE)	microsoft.com/learning/en-us/private-cloud-certification.aspx
CompTIA Cloud+	certification.comptia.org/getCertified/certifications/cloudplus.aspx
HP Vertica Big Data Certifications	my.vertica.com/resources/certification
Cloudera Certified Professional - Data Scientist (CCP - DS)	cloudera.com/content/cloudera/en/training/certification/ccp-ds.html
Microsoft Certified Solutions Developer (MCSD)	microsoft.com/learning/en-us/mcsd-certification.aspx
Adobe Certified Expert (ACE) For Developers	adobe.com/support/certification/developer.html
(ISC)2 Certified Secure Software Lifecycle Professional (CSSLP)	isc2.org/csslp/Default.aspx
Google Apps For Business Certified Deployment Specialist (CDS)	certification.googleapps.com/Home
C and C++ Certifications	cppinstitute.org/?p=5

INFORMATION TECHNOLOGY

Certification/License	Resource
Amazon Web Services - Certified Solutions Architect (AWS)	globalknowledge.com/us-en/training/certification-prep/brands/aws/section/ solutions-architect/aws-certified-solutions-architect-associate
HDI Support Center Analyst (HDI-SCA)	thinkhdi.com/education/courses/hdi-support-center-analyst.aspx#
Apple Certified Support Professional (ACSP)	training.apple.com/certification/osxyosemite
iET Service Desk Analyst & Service Desk Manager	iet-solutions.com//index.php?cID=252
Microsoft Specialist in Windows 10 - Configuring Windows Devices	microsoft.com/en-us/learning/specialist-certification.aspx
CompTIA A+	certification.comptia.org/getCertified/certifications/a.aspx
ACMT - Apple Certified Macintosh Technician	training.apple.com/certification/acmt
CompTIA Server+	certification.comptia.org/getCertified/certifications/server.aspx
Wireless - Cisco Certified Network Professional Wireless (CCNP)	cisco.com/web/learning/certifications/professional/ccnp_wireless/index.html
Citrix Certified Professional - Mobility (CCP-M)	training.citrix.com/cms/index.php/certification/mobility-certification/
CompTIA Mobility+	certification.comptia.org/getCertified/certifications/mobilityplus.aspx
CompTIA Security+	certification.comptia.org/certifications/security
Certified Ethical Hacker (CEH)	eccouncil.org/Certification/certified-ethical-hacker
SANS GIAC Security Essentials (GSEC)	giac.org/certification/security-essentials-gsec
Certified Information Systems Security Professional (CISSP)	isc2.org/CISSP/Default.aspx
Certified Information Security Manager (CISM)	isaca.org/Certification/CISM-Certified-Information-Security-Manager/Pages/default.aspx
DRI International's Certified Business Continuity Professional (CBCP)	drii.org/certification/cbcp.php
Business Continuity Institute's Certification of the BCI (CBCI)	thebci.org/index.php/training-education/certification
Mile 2's Certified Disaster Recovery Engineer (C/DRE)	mile2.com/disaster-recovery-business-continuity-planning.html
Information Technology Information Library (ITIL)	axelos.com/best-practice-solutions/itil
Agile Certified Practitioner (PMI-ACP)	pmi.org/certifications/types/agile-acp

INFORMATION TECHNOLOGY

Appendix B – Salary Considerations

Got to the salary stage of the interview! Salary negotiations are tricky and sensitive. Don't sweat, but be prepared. Research a fair salary. Understand the benchmarks for your position. Arm yourself with salary information. Spend adequate time conducting research to find out average salary ranges for similar jobs in the area, industry, and geography. Then decide on an appropriate salary range. To determine a realistic salary range, forego any thoughts about how many kids you have in college, your boat payment, or your upcoming European vacation. Instead, research and calculate an appropriate salary. It is also good practice to identify your "can't live with" point. Think about the reasons why you would not be willing to accept a lower amount. Many websites offer ideas on how to establish these salary points. If at a loss, a few ideas are presented below which offer some insights to consider.

Determine the average salary for your position at your desired location. By way of example for other occupations, Figure B-1 was developed from 2016 United States salary statistics from Salary.com for Systems Administrators and Web App Developers at three different locations. Study the table and cross check other sources to provide you salary expectations. Remember, title, experience and certification are all variables and the table below is given as a guide.

Position	Location	10%	25%	50%	75%	90%
Systems Administrator II	Tampa, FL	$53,961	$62,181	$71,209	$80,185	$88,356
Systems Administrator II	San Francisco, CA	$69,697	$80,314	$91,976	$103,569	$114,123
Systems Administrator II	El Paso, TX	$46,931	$54,080	$61,932	$69,738	$76,845
Web App Developer I	Tampa, FL	$45,918	$49,757	$53,973	$61,488	$68,330
Web App Developer I	San Francisco, CA	$59,310	$64,267	$69,713	$79,420	$88,258
Web App Developer I	El Paso, TX	$39,936	$43,275	$46,941	$53,478	$59,429

Figure B-1 | 2016 Sample Salary Averages for Systems Administrator II and Web Application Developer I

Look for variables

Certifications and Experience may improve your salary threshold. Often, employers will pay more for certification. Sometimes, certification is the only way to get your foot in the door. The goodness of certifications is that it differentiates you in the marketplace and gives you a competitive advantage in the job market; or may get you into the interview.

Remember, you may experience salary increases because of both certification and because of your prior military experience. There is no guaranteeing a higher salary for certification and experience, but you can certainly use these as a basis for negotiation.

Appendix C – Personal Strategic Roadmap

Personal Strategic Road Map v1.0

GR8MilitaryPM ®

Vision: Obtain A Project Management career that meets or exceeds my expectations

Mission: Develop a course of action to create a satisfying and financially lucrative transitional outcome.

Transition Date:

RoadMap Initiation Date:

IMPROVEMENTS

ASSESSMENT RESULTS ➡ Areas for Change/Improvement from Star Chart results outside the pentagon

	Change / Improvement # 1	Change / Improvement #2	Change / Improvement #3	Change / Improvement #4
1. Environmental/Spousal				
2. Characteristics				
3. Timing				
4. Skills				
5. Market Place	□ Commercial □ Contract □ Civil Service			

VISION

VISION:

Based upon your reading and the five assessment areas above, restate your job objectives to include some or all of the following: Job place/location (CONUS/OCONUS, state/city, timeframe, marketplace focus, salary range, possible positions, risk level you are willing to take, industries, and any other considerations

YOUR VISION:

GOALS & ACHIEVEMENT

GOALS:

Pick most important improvement areas from above you want to focus on, depending on level of complexity, learning, or duration (i.e., school).

* List: goals, align which Assessment it ties, year/quarter/month expected to achieve, and present your achievement path (how you will get to your goal and possible steps if necessary

PRIORITY	GOAL STATEMENT	ASSESSMENT TIE	PATH TO ACHIEVING GOAL	YEAR/QTR/MO TO ACHIEVE (personally set)	ACHIEVED ?
GOAL # 1	enter goal here...	Environment / Characteristics / Timing / Skills / Market Place	enter steps....		YES / NO Reschedule or no longer need? Date
GOAL # 2		Environment / Characteristics / Timing / Skills / Market Place			YES / NO Reschedule or no longer need? Date
GOAL # 3		Environment / Characteristics / Timing / Skills / Market Place			YES / NO Reschedule or no longer need? Date
GOAL # 4		Environment / Characteristics / Timing / Skills / Market Place			YES / NO Reschedule or no longer need? Date

ATTEST

Date of Next Review:

Signature: _____ Date:

Spouse Signature: _____ Date:

Gr8MilitaryPM.com

©Copyright 2014

Acknowledgements

I would like to express my gratitude to the many outstanding people I had the good fortune to come in contact during my military career that provided the platform for my success, which has led to a burning desire to share some insight with the next generation of transitioning Service members.

I wish to thank SGM (R) Johnny Myers for his editing and my coauthor Jay Hicks for his dedication to provide transitioning Service members a template for success. Most importantly I want to thank the officers, noncommissioned officers and Service members that have provided invaluable contributions to my development, as well as my family; my wife Gloria, sons Brian and Kevin, daughter-in-law Tanja, and granddaughters Destiny and Jordan.

The TRANSITIONING COMBAT ARMS PROFESSIONAL provides a proverbial bridge to the brave Soldiers and Marines that have dedicated their lives in defense of our great nation. Their support for America, must continue to be compensated with our unending support for them and their families.

Jack L. Tilley
12th Sergeant Major of the Army
Retired

Writing is never a solitary act. Collaborating with Sergeant Majors Jack Tilley and Johnny Myers on this very special project has been nothing but inspirational. Partnership always makes for a better product, and they have been superb partners.

It is very rewarding to work with those who are in transition and know they have a very lucrative future in the civilian world. I am blessed with so many friends and colleagues who live and believe in the mission to assist veterans. They have helped selflessly, without pause, and I am forever thankful for their encouragement and their desire to see this mission continue.

I am grateful to those who have shared their stories for this book. Some special thanks go to Sandy and Jeff Lawrence, who both offered great insight and direction. I am thankful for those who spent countless hours reviewing this work, especially Bill Livingston, YC and Rachel Parris, Mark Ellington, Dennis Barletta, Cam Miles, AKA "The Nitpicker," and Chip Apple.

Wising you a successful and lucrative transition!

Jay Hicks
Gr8Transitions4U

End Notes

Chapter 1

1   Powell's Autobiography

2   "Mind Tools Editorial Team, Bridges' Transition Model", *https://mind-tools.com/pages/article/bridges-transition-model.htm,* (accessed April 15, 2016).

Chapter 2

1   http://themilitarywallet.com/military-retirement-pay-enough-retire/

2   Henry, Todd, "Die Empty", (Portfolio / Penguin NY, New York, 2013), 4.

3   Gottreu, Scott, "The Difference Between Occupation & Vocation", January 09, 2012, *http://codeoffaith.com/804/the-difference-between-oc-cupation-vocation,* (accessed May 2, 2016).

4   Henry, Todd, "The Accidental Creative", (Portfolio / Penguin NY, New York, 2011), 210.

5   Christopher, Shane, "Why are employers Seeking Military Experience", G.I. Jobs, April 28, 2014, *http://gijobs.com/employers-seeking-military-experience*, (accessed April 15, 2016).

6   Biro, Meghan, "5 Reasons Leaders Hire Veterans", Forbes, November 4, 2012, *http://forbes.com/sites/meghanbiro/2012/11/04/5-reasons-leaders-hire-veterans*, (accessed April 15, 2016).

7   Society of Human Resource Managers, "Employing Military Personnel and Recruiting Veterans, What HR can do," SHRM, June 23, 2010, *http://shrm.org/research/surveyfindings/documents/10-531%20 military%20program%20report_fnl.pdf*, (accessed June 25, 2015).

8   Military Friendly, "Top 100", Military Friendly, 2015, *http://militaryfriendly.com/top-100*, (accessed April 15, 2016).

9   Forbes, "Top 10 Military Friendly Employers", http://forbes.com/pictures/efkk45lkjh/top-10-military-friendly-employers, 2016, (accessed April 15, 2016)

10   https://resumegenius.com/how-to-write-a-resume/skills-section-writing-guide

11   http://nvti.ucdenver.edu/resources/resourcelibrary/pdfs/strengths.pdf

12   collinsdictionary.com/us/dictionary/english/soft-skills

13   http://job-hunt.org/veterans-job-search/military-soft-skill-advantage.shtml

14   http://journals.sagepub.com/doi/pdf/10.1177/1080569912460400

15   U.S Department of Veteran's Affairs, "Education and Training", *http://benefits.va.gov/gibill/post911_gibill.asp*, (accessed May 2, 2016).

16   Lerner, Michele, "How big should your emergency fund be?" Bankrate. com, Mar 6, 2012, http://bankrate.com/finance/savings/how-big-should-emergency-fund-be.aspx (accessed May 2, 2016).

17   Caarl S. Savino and Ronald L. Krannich, Ph.D., "The Military to Civilian Transition Guide, secrets to finding a great jobs and employers", (Competitive Edge Services, 2014-2015 edition), 42.

18   Doyle, Alison, "Resume Types: Chronological, Functional, Combination", About.com, 2015, http://jobsearch.about.com/od/resumes/p/resumetypes.htm, (accessed May 2, 2016).

19   Savino and Krannich, "The Military to Civilian Transition Guide", 10.

20 Hicks, Jay, "Bullet Proof Your Resume", LinkedIn, *https://linkedin.com/ pulse/bullet-proof-your-resume-jay-hicks-pmp?trk=pulse_spock-articles*, (accessed May 2, 2016).

21 Hicks, Jay, "Do you have a 'Killer Cover Letter'?", LinkedIn, *https://linkedin.com/pulse/transitioning-military-service-members- do-you-have-cover-hicks-pmp?trk=pulse_spock-articles*, (accessed May 2, 2016).

Chapter 3

1   https://wallethub.com/edu/best-cities-for-jobs/2173/

2   U.S. Department of Veterans Affairs, "Education and Training", March 2015, http://benefits.va.gov/gibill/licensing_certification.asp, (accessed May 5, 2016).

3   https://bls.gov/oes/current/oes230000.htm#st

4   http://americanlawyer.com/id=1202766638199/Legal-Industry-Job-Growth-Remains-Flat?slreturn=20170115052628

5   http://forbes.com/sites/kathryndill/2015/05/21/the-10-best-and-worst-paying-jobs-in-sales-right-now/#78c6ebc166f8

6   http://ncmahq.org/discover-our-profession/career-path/skills-to-enter-the-profession

7   http://investopedia.com/articles/financial-careers/08/financial-ca-reer-options-professionals.asp?lgl=bnull-right-rail-partial-sticky

8   http://thinkadvisor.com/2012/05/23/8-fast-growing-financial-ser-vices-jobs

9   http://degreesfinder.com/information-online-degree-programs/mil-itary/translating-intelligence-experience-to-the-civilian-world/

10 https://intelligencecareers.gov/icmembers.html

11 https://recruiter.com/careers/intelligence-analysts/outlook/

12 https://bls.gov/ooh/business-and-financial/market-research-analysts.htm

13 https://sokanu.com/careers/detective/

14 https://sokanu.com/careers/detective/

15 http://icaschool.com/?utm_source=bing&utm_medium=cpc&utm_campaign=State%20Specific%20%28License%20Required%29&utm_term=home%20inspection%20%2Btraining&utm_content=Home%20Inspectors

16 http://degreesfinder.com/information-online-degree-programs/military/translating-intelligence-experience-to-the-civilian-world/

17 https://onetonline.org/link/summary/11-2011.00

18 http://nber.org/digest/oct03/w9633.html

19 https://bls.gov/ooh/management/

20 https://bls.gov/ooh/management/

21 https://bls.gov/oes/current/oes111021.htm

22 https://bls.gov/ooh/management/lodging-managers.htm

23 http://degreesfinder.com/information-online-degree-programs/military/translating-intelligence-experience-to-the-civilian-world/

24 https://pmi.org/about/learn-about-pmi/who-are-project-managers

25 Hicks, Cobb, The Transitioning Military Project Manager.

26 http://work.colum.edu/~amiller/pr-education.htm

27 "Occupational Outlook Handbook: Logistics," Bureau of Labor Statistics, Department of Labor, January 8, 2014, http://bls.gov/ooh/business-and-financial/logisticians.htm#tab-1, (accessed June 25, 2015).

28 "How To Find The Right Training For A Career As A Mechanic", Truck Drivers Salary, 2015, http://truckdriversalary.net/mechanic-school, (accessed June 30, 2015).

29 glassdoor, "Information Technology Salaries in United States", *https://glassdoor.com/Salaries/us-information-technology-salary-SRCH_IL.0,2_IN1_KO3,25.htm*, (accessed May 5, 2016).

30 Bureau of Labor Statistics, "Occupational Handbook – Computer and Information Technology – Software Developers", December 17, 2015, http://bls.gov/careeroutlook/2015/article/projections-occupation.htm, (accessed May 2, 2016).

31 Bureau of Labor Statistics, "Occupational Handbook – Computer and Information Systems Managers", December 17, 2015, http://bls.gov/ooh/management/computer-and-information-systems-managers.htm, (accessed April 15, 2016).

32 Toolbox.com, "A 2015 Outlook for VoIP", January 2015, http://it.toolbox.com/blogs/voip-news/a-2015-outlook-for-voip-65283, (accessed May 5, 2016).

33 Juniper, "Juniper Networks Certification Program", March 2016, *https://juniper.net/us/en/training/certification*, (accessed May 5, 2016).

34 Bureau of Labor Statistics, "Occupational Handbook – Computer and Information Technology – Software Developers", December 17, 2015, *http://bls.gov/ooh/computer-and-information-technology/software-developers.htm*, (accessed April 15, 2016).

35 Study.com, "Software Developer: Educational Requirements & Career Info", 2016, *http://study.com/articles/Software_Developer_Educational_Requirements_for_a_Computer_Software_Engineer.html*, (accessed May 5, 2016).

36 Letteer, Ray. "The Transitioning Military Cybersecurity Professional." Gr8Transitions4U: Tampa, FL (Forthcoming, December 2016).

37 Infosec Institute, "Average Certified Ethical Hacker (CEH) Salary 2016", 2016, *http://resources.infosecinstitute.com/certified-ethical-hacker-salary*, (accessed May 5, 2016).

38 Letteer, Ray. "The Transitioning Military Cybersecurity Professional." Gr8Transitions4U: Tampa, FL (Forthcoming, December 2016).

39 Bureau of Labor Statistics, "Occupational Handbook – Computer and Information Systems Managers", December 17, 2015, http://bls.gov/ooh/management/computer-and-information-systems-managers.htm, (accessed April 15, 2016).

40 National Defense University - Information Resource Management College – iCollege, "Catalog and Student Handbook 2015-2016", 2015, *http://icollege.ndu.edu/Portals/74/Documents/NDUiCollege2016CatalogWEB%20(1).pdf*, (accessed May 5, 2016).

41 Staff, "Defense Acquisition Workforce Improvement Act (DAWIA)", December 18, 2013, *http://dau.mil/doddacm/Pages/Certification.aspx*, (accessed May 2, 2016).

42 Staff, "Defense Acquisition University", December 18, 2013, *http://icatalog.dau.mil/onlinecatalog/CareerLvl.aspx*, (accessed May 2, 2016).

43 Staff, "Defense Acquisition University", December 18, 2013, *http://icatalog.dau.mil/onlinecatalog/CareerLvl.aspx*, (accessed May 2, 2016).

44 ArmyReal.com, "Army e-Learning Program", 2016, *http://armyreal.com/resources/item/890*, (accessed May 2, 2016).

Chapter 4

1   Ledford, Tranette, "The Best Jobs: Government Employee or Government Contractor?" ClearanceJobs, July 25, 2010, *http://news.clearancejobs.com/2010/07/25/the-best-jobs-government-employee-or-government-contractor/*, (accessed May 2, 2016).

2   Ledford, Tranette, "The Best Jobs: Government Employee or Government Contractor?" ClearanceJobs, July 25, 2010, *http://news.clearancejobs.com/2010/07/25/the-best-jobs-government-employee-or-government-contractor/*, (accessed May 2, 2016).

3   Ledford, Tranette, "The Best Jobs: Government Employee or Government Contractor?" ClearanceJobs, July 25, 2010, *http://news.clearancejobs.com/2010/07/25/the-best-jobs-government-employee-or-government-contractor/*, (accessed May 2, 2016).

4   Zach Shen, "The Best Places to Work in the Federal Government 2013 Rankings", Partnership for Public Service, June 14, 2013, *http://bestplacestowork.org/BPTW/rankings/governmentwide,*

5   USA.gov, "Pay and Benefits for Federal Employees", *https://usa.gov/benefits-for-federal-employees#item-36407*, (accessed May 2, 2016).

6   Stone, Adam, "Breaking down pros & cons of public & private sectors", Navy Times, March 26, 2014, *http://navytimes.com/article/20140326/JOBS/303260044/Breaking-down-pros-cons-public-private-sectors/* (accessed May 2, 2016).

7   John Cibinic, Jr. and Ralph C. Nash, Jr., Administration of Government Contracts, The George Washington University, Government Contracts Program, National Law Center, Washington D.C., Third Edition, 1995

8   Ledford, Tranette, "The Best Jobs: Government Employee or Government Contractor?" ClearanceJobs, July 25, 2010, *http://news.clearancejobs.com/2010/07/25/the-best-jobs-government-employee-or-government-contractor/*, (accessed May 2, 2016).

9   Stone, Adam, "Breaking down pros & cons of public & private sectors", Navy Times, March 26, 2014, *http://navytimes.com/article/20140326/JOBS/303260044/Breaking-down-pros-cons-public-private-sectors,* (accessed May 2, 2016).

10 IRS, "Tax Information for Retirement Plans", *irs.gov/Retirement-Plans,* (accessed May 2, 2016).

11 Staff, "The Stark difference between private and public sector ERP implementations, Panorama Consulting Solutions", September 13, 2013, *http://panorama-consulting.com/the-stark-difference-between-private-and-public-sector-erp-implementations/*, (accessed May 2, 2016).

12 Federal Salary Council Working Group, "Report of Federal Salary Council Working Group", September 4, 2014, *http://govexec.com/media/gbc/docs/pdfs_edit/101714kl2.pdf*, (accessed June 21, 2016)

13 Morgan, Richard, "Five Mandatory Benefits for Full-Time Employees", 2016, Houston Chronical, *http://smallbusiness.chron.com/five-mandatory-benefits-fulltime-employees-18874.html*, (accessed June 21, 2016).

14 Great Place to Work, "PricewaterhouseCoopers LLP", 2016, *http://us.greatrated.com/pwc/great-perks*, (accessed May 2, 2016).

15 Hay Group, "The Best Places to Work in the Federal Government 2013 Rankings", Partnership for Public Service, June 14, 2013, *http://bestplacestowork.org/BPTW/overview/analysis/private_sector_comparison.php*, (accessed May 2, 2016).

The Military Transitioning Series

The Transitioning Military Series helps service members evaluate and understand their potential to transform themselves into a marketable commodity within both public and private sectors. Each career-based book enables the translation of military experience to the commercial world. Read and use each of these books as a reference to guide during your transition. Insight is provided for those seeking the most satisfying job beyond their military career, with real-world success stories.

A unique combination of features offered through this book series include:

- Career Mapping and Translation
- Commercial Market Exploration
- Transitional Preparedness
- Individual Assessments
- Personal Strategic Roadmap

Interested in another career field? Check out our other books on career field transition for the military:

| Project Manager | Logistician | Information Technology | Cybersecurity Professional |

Jay Hicks and Sandy Cobb are dedicated to providing insight and guidance for those looking to transition successfully from the Military with the least amount of stress. Both Jay and Sandy speak around the U.S. in support of transition as well as career field insight, and are available for conferences, podcasts, webinars, and training. For more information on upcoming events and new releases, visit: GR8Transitions4U.com.

69279353R00114

Made in the USA
Lexington, KY
28 October 2017